# TALENT MANAGEMENT

# TALENT MANAGEMENT: BASICS

Question

How important do you think talent management is for your organization?

Options:

1. Very important
2. Fairly important
3. Not important

Answer

**Option 1:** *Giving proper weight to the goal of managing the talent in your organization effectively is a very important first step. You can use this course to build on your knowledge of how to acquire and nurture talent.*

**Option 2:** *People and their skills are tremendously valuable resources. As a manager, you have to know how to acquire and build talent to get the best results for your organization.*

**Option 3:** *Even organizations with relatively unskilled employees need to be able to manage them effectively. High turnover is costly, and failing to attract and develop talent limits success and productivity.*

Because talent is a valuable and sometimes scarce commodity, talent management is becoming increasingly important.

To succeed, organizations attract, develop, and retain talented individuals.

When talent is well managed, the success of your department grows, and this, in turn, leads to greater competitiveness for your organization.

In this course, you'll learn why talent management is important and what its benefits are. You'll also be introduced to the four key components of talent management – planning, acquiring, developing, and retaining talent.

The course will also help you recognize and fulfill your role in managing talent. This involves implementing vital strategies for recruiting, motivating, and assessing talent, as well as creating a supportive work environment in which talent can thrive.

**Introduction to Talent Management**

1. The Importance of Talent Management
2. The Components of Talent Management
3. The Manager's Role in Talent Management

# THE IMPORTANCE OF TALENT MANAGEMENT

1. What is talent management?

Most people agree that employees are vital to a company's success. But it's not enough to say that people are important. Organizations need to be designed and managed in ways that optimize the attraction, retention, and performance of talented individuals. This approach is strategic in that it involves making decisions about how to manage human capital in a way that takes into account the organization's needs.

So the decisions you make about employees – whether in hiring, developing, or retaining them – will shape your organization's competencies and its ultimate success.

That's where talent management comes in.

Talent management is an ongoing process for recruiting, developing, and retaining talented individuals to meet current and future business needs and objectives. It helps a company stay competitive.

Talent management isn't succession planning, replacement planning, or succession management. Although it's related to these areas, talent management takes a broader approach.

**Succession planning**

Succession planning focuses on identifying employees within an organization who can fill key positions in the future.

## Replacement planning

Replacement planning focuses on identifying individuals within an organization who can assume key positions if the employees currently in those positions leave – either over the long term or as just a short-term measure.

## Succession management

Succession management focuses on daily preparation of employees earmarked for future promotion to key positions.

Question

What do you think the ultimate goal of talent management is?

**Options:**

1. To help an organization achieve its strategic business objectives
2. To save on employment costs
3. To retain talented employees
4. To ensure an organization gets the maximum amount of work from employees

Answer

**Option 1:** *This is the correct option. The overarching goal of talent management is to help an organization achieve its strategic business objectives.*

**Option 2:** *This option is incorrect. A good talent management strategy should save on employment costs. However, this isn't the ultimate goal of talent management, which has a much broader focus.*

**Option 3:** *This option is incorrect. Every talent management strategy should include plans for retaining talented employees. However, the overarching goal of talent management is to help an organization meet its strategic business objectives.*

**Option 4:** *This option is incorrect. The ultimate goal of talent management is to help an organization achieve its strategic business objectives. It's goal is broader than getting the maximum amount of work from employees.*

## 2. Talent management practices

The goal of talent management is to help an organization meet its objectives. Because objectives vary, the way talent management is defined and implemented varies from company to company. But typical talent management practices include performance management, learning and training, leadership development, career planning, recruitment, engagement, and compensation and rewards.

However you define and implement talent management practices, you should ensure that they are readily understood by everyone in your organization.

This is important because talent management isn't the sole reserve of the HR Department – it's relevant to all those who are involved and affected by it.

And although you may not be able to apply all talent management practices to all employees in the organization, you can at least apply some practices consistently across the organization.

**Lila**

"My company is rapidly expanding into the global market, so gaining more talent is crucial to us. Also we market ourselves as having better talent than our competitors. So our talent management strategy relies heavily on recruiting the top talent available and assimilating this talent. We use intensive, ongoing training, top rewards, and a range of outplacement options."

**Graham**

"My company is consolidating its resources so it can focus on providing the most cost-effective solutions. So we see talent management largely in terms of identifying top performers, acknowledging and rewarding employees who improve production processes, and developing leaders.

We identify what talent is needed, draw that talent from our own ranks or outsource it, manage the development of our employees with demand in mind, and then try to control the retention of employees so little new recruitment is needed."

Now that you have a sense of what talent management is, the next question to answer is "who is the talent?" At the most basic level, the answer is everyone who performs an organization's work – including both part-time and full-time employees.

Talent can include people in pivotal roles - like specialists in engineering, manufacturing, support, customer service, or sales.

And talent can encompass not only people who can be promoted to management, but also people who can take on more responsibility as individual professional contributors.

Question

Which are key concepts related to talent management?

**Options:**

1. It's a process for the recruitment, development, and retention of talent
2. How it's implemented changes according to a company's needs, goals, and strategies
3. It includes both full-time and part-time employees
4. Its purpose is to promote an organization's strategic objectives
5. All talent management activities need to be applied to all employees
6. It should focus on preparing only individuals with high potential for management roles

Answer

**Option 1:** *This option is correct. Talent management is an ongoing process that involves identifying, acquiring, developing, and retaining talent in a way that supports an organization's objectives.*

**Option 2:** *This option is correct. Every organization needs to tailor its definition and implementation of talent management to its specific needs. So each talent management plan should be designed to fit the organization and its changing needs.*

**Option 3:** *This is a correct option. In the broadest sense, talent in-*

cludes all full-time and part-time employees who are assigned work and held accountable for it. Some organizations may take a more narrow focus and concentrate on only senior executives. And in other organizations, individuals in key roles or with high potential may get special attention.

**Option 4:** *This option is correct. The aim of talent management is to help an organization achieve its strategic objectives. So it should help the organization grow in a direction that'll maximize the company's competitiveness within the marketplace.*

**Option 5:** *This option is incorrect. It may not be reasonable to expect an organization to apply all talent management practices to all employees. In some cases, it may be better to apply some practices consistently across the organization.*

**Option 6:** *This option is incorrect. Talent management may also focus on individuals who are ready to take on more responsibility as individual professional contributors.*

3. Business environment challenges

To understand its importance, it helps to consider what happens when you go without talent management. Typically, you can end up with mismatches between supply and demand – either having too many employees, resulting in layoffs and restructuring, or having too little talent and not being able to achieve your objectives successfully.

A talent management strategy also helps you overcome key business environment challenges – such as globalization, increased competition, and increased knowledge requirements.

**Globalization**

With globalization and technologies like the Internet, companies from all over the world compete for the same employees.

Employees can also more easily take up new positions in companies across the globe, and have greater career mobility. So finding and keeping the best talent needs strong and effective strategies.

**Increased competition**

Increased marketplace competition requires organizations to perform consistently well so as to hold their market shares. To maintain these standards, companies need to hire and retain the best talent.

Increased competition also leads to a highly volatile marketplace. So organizations need to know the strengths of their workforces and respond quickly to changes in labor and product demand.

**Increased knowledge requirements**

To meet increased knowledge requirements, organizations need new hires who can quickly assimilate knowledge and new technologies.

They also need experienced employees, who have in-depth knowledge of their industries and good leadership and mentoring skills. Demand for skills and leadership is outstripping supply – when experienced people retire, it's difficult to find suitably qualified people to replace them.

So competition for employees who have the necessary qualifications, skills, and leadership abilities is fierce.

Question

Which characteristics of the current business environment make talent management especially important?

**Options:**

1. Employers compete globally for talented employees
2. Companies have to react to change quickly and maintain high standards to keep their market shares
3. Businesses need experienced leadership as well as employees who can adapt to changing technologies
4. Employees increasingly make lifetime commitments to a single employment path
5. Businesses are under pressure to implement environmentally sustainable practices

Answer

**Option 1:** *This option is correct. With globalization, employers from all over the world have to compete for the same employees. It's also easier for employees to take up new positions in other regions or countries. This makes it harder to recruit and retain suitably skilled employees.*

**Option 2:** *This is a correct option. Increased competition places pressure on organizations to perform well and to do so consistently in a rapidly changing business environment. To do this, companies need to hire and retain the best talent.*

**Option 3:** *This option is correct. Increased knowledge requirements mean that companies need employees who can readily adapt to new technologies, as well as experienced employees who can provide leadership.*

**Option 4:** *This option is incorrect. Rapid changes due to globalization, competition, and emerging technology mean that employees have greater career mobility than in the past.*

**Option 5:** *This option is incorrect. There may be increased pressure on businesses to implement environmentally sustainable practices, but this isn't one of the key challenges that talent management has to address.*

4. Key benefits

Effective talent management can help an organization meet the challenges of the modern business environment. It can also directly benefit both employees and the organization itself.

There are a number of benefits that talent management brings to an organization:

- increased productivity and capability
- increased commitment from valued employees, and
- reduced turnover of employees

**Increased productivity**

Part of a good talent management program is a strategy to engage and thereby retain employees. Talent management encourages employees to develop their capabilities and, in turn, improve their productivity. It engages employees through such practices as coaching and mentoring, as well as by offering training and learning opportunities.

When you hang on to talented employees with practices like these, you don't have to continuously train and orient new hires, or take the risk that new hires will be unable to meet job requirements.

**Increased commitment**

No company wants to lose valued employees. Good talent management improves employee morale and has a positive influence on company culture.

Talent management should empower employees. It encourages people to assume greater responsibility, to take risks, and to achieve more. This increases valued employees' commitment to the organization and helps it retain top talent.

**Reduced turnover**

Good talent management reduces a company's rate of employee turnover. As their turnover decreases, businesses spend less on hiring and suffer fewer drops in productivity when training new hires.

Another benefit of reduced turnover is that compensation paid for talent developed within an organization is typically lower than compensation paid to new hires. Businesses save money by holding on to talented and experienced employees.

The benefits of talent management for employees include higher motivation and commitment, career development, increased knowledge about and contribution to company goals, and sustained motivation and job satisfaction.

**Arlene**

"I joined my company very recently, and management's interest in my potential is just amazing. I completed some personality tests to help me find direction within the company. I've been given several exciting training opportunities. Also, I have a mentor who's helping me develop an in-depth understanding of the business, where I can fit in, and how I can contribute to my company's success.

This really motivates me to get up and come in to work in the morning. I feel like my career can develop here."

**Joel**

"Over the years with this company, I've grown and developed. The company provides me with fresh challenges and support that keeps me motivated, even after all this time.

I know how my contribution affects company goals and this makes me feel really connected to its successes and failures. So I'm invested in the company and the company invests in me too – developing my career and really rewarding the work I put in."

**Tina**

"I started out at the bottom in this company, but my managers paid attention to how hard I worked, and noticed and developed my talents. They helped me build a real career here.

My suggestions helped to reduce unnecessary expenditure and boosted product quality. At another company, my voice might not have been heard. Knowing how valued my contribution is really motivates me to do more and learn more. I guess that's why I love my job."

Question

What can talent management do for organizations and for employees?

**Options:**

1. Enable a company to maintain higher levels of productivity
2. Reduce expenditures related to employee turnover
3. Encourage employees to support company goals
4. Improve employees' commitment to their work
5. Encourage valued employees to stay with the organ-

ization

6. Ensure all talented employees are fast-tracked for management positions
7. Reduce the need for employee compensation and reward incentives

Answer

*Option 1:* This option is correct. When you retain talented employees, you don't have to continuously train and orient new hires, or take the risk that new hires will be unable to meet job requirements - all of which decrease productivity.

*Option 2:* This is a correct option. An organizational benefit of talent management is reduced employee turnover, which saves on costs and improves productivity.

*Option 3:* This option is correct. Talent management benefits employees by increasing their knowledge about and contribution to organizational goals.

*Option 4:* This is a correct option. Talent management provides sustained motivation and job satisfaction for employees, because it helps them take ownership of their work, and express their aptitudes and interests more fully.

*Option 5:* This option is correct. Organizations benefit from talent management through increased commitment from valued employees, because their careers are developed and they receive better training.

*Option 6:* This option is incorrect. Often the goal with talented employees is to increase their responsibilities, rather than simply promoting them to management positions.

*Option 7:* This option is incorrect. Companies do need to reward and adequately compensate employees to retain the best talent.

5. Summary

Talent management is an ongoing process that involves identifying, acquiring, developing, and retaining talent in support of an organization's goals. How talent management is defined and implemented depends on the goals of a company and on the different talent pools identified.

Effective talent management can help organizations overcome challenges associated with the modern business environment. These include challenges related to globalization, increased competition, and increased knowledge requirements.

# THE COMPONENTS OF TALENT MANAGEMENT

1. Ownership of talent management

Having talent means being able to do something exceptionally well. But talent isn't enough on its own. It requires the opportunity to practice and hone your skills, in an environment that enables you to do this. So managing talent is about giving people the opportunity to demonstrate and develop their talents, as well as directing and guiding these skills.

Question

Who do you think should take responsibility for talent management in your organization?

**Options:**

1. The Human Resources Department
2. Senior Managers
3. The board
4. Line managers
5. Peers
6. Consultants

Answer

**Option 1:** *This option is correct. HR should certainly develop a talent management policy, though it has to be supported and implemented by managers and other decision makers to be effective.*

**Option 2:** This option is correct. Senior management and other decision makers need to put a sound talent management policy in place, and play a role in implementing some of its components.

**Option 3:** This option is correct. Decision makers need to understand the importance of talent management, and put their weight behind it, so organizations plan adequately – and invest sufficiently – in the processes of managing talent.

**Option 4:** This option is correct. Line managers have a significant role to play in developing and retaining talent in any organization. They bring the talent management practices to the ground level.

**Option 5:** This option is incorrect. Talent management has to be implemented by managers, Human Resource Departments, and decision makers to be effective.

**Option 6:** This option is incorrect. Talent management has to be part of an organization's planning, decision-making, and day-to-day management, so it can't be outsourced to consultants.

You should consider how the talent management process will be governed in an organization – in other words, who will be accountable for it. You might give ownership to the Human Resources Department but this could result in limited buy-in from other parts of the organization, as those departments might assume it's something HR does in isolation.

A more effective approach could be for HR to put a process in place, making sure it's consistent and fair. This process would have to be supported from the top of the organization and implemented by managers throughout the organization.

For an effective talent management process, there needs to be buy-in from the board down.

If the board and management are actively involved, the four components of talent management can be integrated throughout an organization more effectively.

These components are planning, acquiring, developing, and retaining talent.

## 2. Talent planning

Without a good plan, it's hard to channel resources - like time, money, and effort - where they're most needed. So the first step in talent management is to come up with guidelines for action.

The talent planning process can be broken into several steps. First, you establish the organization's requirements - its goals, for example. Then you decide on a focus for talent management and define required competencies related to that focus. Next you establish criteria for assessing, measuring, and developing these competencies. Finally, you conduct talent audits. The planning process can be revisited as the needs of the organization change and develop.

An organization's talent requirements include what it needs right now to be successful, and what it will need in the future.

To establish talent requirements, you work from the organization's vision and its strategic objectives.

Once you know what your organization needs, you can start thinking about what type of talent potential to focus on. You may need to focus specifically on employees with high potential, on overall potential, or on technical potential within your organization.

**High potential**

If you decide that the focus of talent management will be on individuals with high potential, you need to clearly define what you mean by high potential.

For example, is it people who can take on a leadership role within a certain time period, or those who regularly over-achieve or over-deliver?

In addition to defining high potential, you need to determine how to assess and measure the existing and potential capabilities of the relevant individuals. You should create high-potential criteria against which to measure these individuals.

**Overall potential**

When talent management is focused on overall potential, all employees are recognized as potentially talented. Talent is fostered and developed at each level of the organization, encouraging promotion from within and helping to reduce employee turnover.

By choosing this broad approach, you won't alienate the general population of your organization – a possible side effect of concentrating talent management activity on a small group of people.

Typically, this strategy helps create an inclusive and cooperative organizational culture.

**Technical potential**

Some organizations have specific technical requirements that are critical to success. So they may want to focus talent management efforts on employees with the relevant expert and specialist skills.

For example, if software development is part of the core business, then developing the technical capabilities of software engineers is key. However, it's important to consider other capabilities as well. Developing technical potential is an additional element in the focus of talent management that may be separate from the focus on wider or overall potential.

Whatever potential talents you decide to focus on, you need to define the competencies and capabilities that indicate talent. Once you're clear about what the competencies are, you need to establish criteria for evaluating and measuring them. Finally, you can use these criteria to audit the talent your organization already possesses.

**Defining competencies**

Competencies are lasting individual attributes that cause or predict high levels of performance. The capabilities people can potentially bring to an organization depend on their skills, intelligence, know-how, and personality traits.

Defining competencies is a process of defining the specific, usable talents that your employees need to meet the organization's objectives and strategic goals. For example, an insurance company might choose statistical expertise as a valuable competency.

Defining and clarifying exactly what people can offer your organization enables auditing and goal setting.

**Establishing criteria**

To evaluate, measure, and develop competencies, you need to establish particular criteria for each identified competency.

For example, suppose your insurance company has defined statistical expertise as a valued competency. It's still too broad a concept. How will you quantify and compare people's abilities transparently and consistently?

You need objective criteria – for instance, academic qualifications and in-house statistical tests – to measure competencies effectively.

**Conducting audits**

Once you've identified desirable competencies and established criteria for measuring them, you need to conduct a talent audit to find out how much talent your organization currently has.

An audit may include different types of activities designed to evaluate the level of current competence against talent indicators you have defined.

Depending on the type of talent you are auditing, there are different assessment methods you can choose from. These include, for example, psychometric tests and questionnaires, in-depth interviews, case studies, and analysis of most recent performance reviews.

Suppose you're formalizing talent management for a division within a global natural gas pipeline company. The division's strategic objectives are to focus on leadership development for existing managers, line supervisors, and emerging leaders. In short, you want to accelerate leadership development within the company.

Based on these objectives, you focus on developing individuals who are capable of managing in a context of fast-changing economies and markets, and multiple cultures, and who have excellent communication skills.

Next you begin defining the list of desired competencies. This may include a proven ability to perform in a stressful, fast-changing environment or a need for specific skill sets.

The criteria you use to measure individuals would be related to those competencies. For instance, you assess each employee's experience and suitability for leadership development programs.

Finally, you use these criteria to conduct an actual audit of these numbers. You establish what skills and capabilities already exist within your division and what capabilities are lacking or weak.

Question

Which are key activities carried out in talent management planning?

**Options:**
1. Deciding what the organization needs in order to achieve its vision and strategic objectives
2. Choosing which individuals require talent development
3. Clarifying which capabilities are most important and creating objective measures for these
4. Establish what level of talent exists within the organization
5. Deciding on a specific code of ethics for managing talent within the organization
6. Developing programs for attracting talent

Answer

**Option 1:** *This option is correct. Determining talent requirements in relation to the organization's vision and strategic objectives ensures that talent management activities are aligned with these.*

**Option 2:** *This option is correct. Deciding on the focus for the talent management efforts – whether on a small group of employees with high potential, all employees, or people with a specific technical capability - is a key activity when planning.*

**Option 3:** *This option is correct. Defining competencies is crucial when planning talent management. You then need to establish objective and measurable criteria for these competencies.*

**Option 4:** *This option is correct. You need to conduct a talent audit to establish the organization's talent strengths, weaknesses, and opportunities. Knowing this enables you to plan for future needs.*

**Option 5:** *This option is incorrect. Typically, an organization will already have a general code of ethics. Talent management is not directly concerned with laying down a code of ethics.*

**Option 6:** *This option is incorrect. The planning component of talent management doesn't get into the specific programs required but rather focuses on determining the type of talent needed.*

So planning gives your talent management process a focus. It defines the talent needs of the organization and determines how successfully the organization is currently meeting those needs. Once planning has reached this point, you're ready to begin actively managing the talent in your organization.

3. Acquiring talent

The start of managing talent is acquiring the right kind for your organization. There are four key activities in acquiring talent. These are attracting, recruiting, selecting, and employing.

Attracting talent is all about inspiring people to want to work for your organization so that they apply when positions become vacant. The more people you can attract, the wider your choice of potential employees.

Having a recruiting brand can help. This brand or image reflects the core values of the organization and communicates the advantages of working for the organization.

**Branding for accounting firm**

The firm needs to change its image. It might start marketing itself as an employer of choice, emphasizing the benefits it provides and creating a catchy slogan like "The figures add up!" This may reinvigorate its image as an employer, thereby attracting more talented individuals.

When deciding how to recruit and select talent, it helps to have a defined process. Using a competency-focused approach helps organizations find the right talent for their needs. When you use this approach, you increase the pool of talent your organization can draw on in the future. But having some flexibility with whatever process you use means you're more open to individuals who may not have the specific job requirements but who may nonetheless possess talent that would be valuable to the organization.

Recruiting is about actively sourcing potential candidates to fill particular vacancies. For example, placing an advertisement in a newspaper is a common way of recruiting people.

However, more effective methods include online recruiting through company web sites and search engines, and personal referrals.

Selecting is about choosing the best candidate to employ. There are usually multiple steps to follow, such as interviews, tests, and background checks.

It's important that candidates experience a fair and timely interviewing and selection process. This ensures that they have a positive perception of the organization.

To help with this, you should have standardized selection criteria and a written hiring process. You need to make decisions based on factual data and consider all qualifications as well as work history.

Employing someone is the process of bringing a person into the organization, or it could mean promoting a person within the organization to a new position. It may also involve outsourcing work through a contracting company.

During this stage, you negotiate a reimbursement package and starting date, and you provide the employee with a positive introduction to the company.

This introduction, sometimes called onboarding, creates lasting impressions. Remember, if employees have an unpleasant experience in the first week of work, they might leave the organization sooner.

Question

Which are key activities for acquiring talent?

**Options:**

1. Becoming a sought-after employer in the job market
2. Using defined competencies to recruit the right kind of talent
3. Choosing between applicants by using a competency-based approach
4. Providing a positive introduction to the organization
5. Training existing personnel to develop their skills
6. Defining what talent means for your organization

Answer

**Option 1:** *This option is correct. Attracting people to want to work for your organization by creating a positive employer brand or image is a key activity for acquiring talent.*

**Option 2:** *This option is correct. Recruiting potential candidates for particular positions is central to bringing talent into an organization.*

**Option 3:** *This option is correct. Selection processes based on competencies can help you find individuals with the talent you need.*

**Option 4:** *This option is correct. Employing people is a key activity for acquiring talent and it involves providing orientation for new* *employees.*

**Option 5:** *This option is incorrect. While skills development is part of talent management, it's not part of the process of acquiring talent.*

**Option 6:** *This option is incorrect. Defining what talent means usually occurs during planning, so that when it comes time to acquire talent, you know what you're looking for.*

4. Developing talent

The fourth component of talent management is developing talent. Strategies for nurturing and building employees' capabilities include career development and training, performance management, and coaching and mentoring.

**Career development and training**

When organizations have programs and training to help people develop their careers, they give motivated employees a chance to improve their abilities.

Very few people have reached their full potential when first recruited. Most employees need and want to grow into their positions. Once aptitudes are identified, you can offer training and career development to develop and enhance employee competencies.

**Performance management**

Performance management encompasses a variety of activities, such as setting goals, giving performance reviews, and providing feedback. It helps employees understand their roles in the context of strategic business objectives.

**Coaching and mentoring**

Coaching and mentoring develop talent by encouraging people to excel at their work and to learn on the job.

If managers are skilled enough to coach and mentor people well, talent can be developed highly effectively. The one-on-one reflective nature of these techniques provides a supportive and intimate quality that can engage people on a more emotional level.

Developing and training have positive spin-offs for retaining talent – when you provide opportunities for advancement or training in new skills, for example, it really helps to motivate and engage employees.

Varied training programs are needed to improve people's performance and skills. And you need to tailor specific programs to help personnel adjust to new technology and upgrade task-specific techniques.

Career development focuses on preparing employees for future work. You can help create individual career action plans for your employees and help them implement those plans.

An effective performance management process can be a motivational tool that drives performance. It helps organizations to effectively manage their employees' performance, and helps them appropriately recognize and reward accomplishments.

**Manage performance**

Performance management helps employees understand what they need to do and why. It includes scheduled discussions of work progress so employees receive the feedback they need to help evaluate their accomplishments and to know where they stand.

A key part of the performance management process is determining how to improve performance. Then you can help employees develop new skills.

The performance management process is important in talent management. Among other things, it identifies competencies and processes for assessment. It also generates performance and potential ratings used for leadership development, compensation, and promotion.

**Recognize and reward**

A key component of performance management is giving performance appraisals. This provides an opportunity to recognize strengths and successes, and to motivate employees to continue improving their performance.

Although pay increases or bonuses are important to employees, praise can go a long way toward making employees feel valued. You can also recognize talented individuals' efforts by assigning them stimulating stretch assignments – so they feel they're valuable contributors.

It's important to remember that to be effective, rewards should be personal or relevant to the employee. Rewards and recognition programs should align with what is most motivating to employees.

Coaching and mentoring are powerful tools for developing and retaining talent.

Talent development doesn't happen just in training courses. Much of it occurs as part of stretching people's roles, using coaching and mentoring as well as appropriate training.

Both mentoring and coaching aim to increase an employee's work-related effectiveness.

But there are some differences in the way that mentoring and coaching work. Mentoring is carried out by an individual who has a track record of success in the area that the person who's mentored wants to improve or learn about. The main role of a mentor is as advice giver.

On the other hand, a coach works with a client to achieve very specific, identifiable goals. The coach and the client are held accountable to the organization to meet those goals.

A coach doesn't provide advice and doesn't "tell" the client what to do. Instead, a coach asks provocative questions to expand the individual's awareness and desire to change.

5. Retaining talent

It's no good investing time, effort, and resources into planning, acquiring, and developing talent if you fail to retain this talent. The longer you can keep talented people in your organization, the greater the return on your investment.

Retaining talent means preventing turnover – or the percentage of employees leaving an organization voluntarily over a specific time span. For example, if 10 out of 100 employees choose to leave an organization in one year, its turnover is 10% per year.

Organizations compete fiercely for talented people, no matter what the economic climate. If an organization doesn't work hard to retain such people, it runs the risk of losing this talent to competitors.

And replacing talented employees who've left can be expensive. Costs include advertising, as well as time spent interviewing and training.

Some strategies that can help retain talent are to provide competitive pay and long-term incentives, provide opportunities for advancement, allow flexible working arrangements, and create a positive work environment.

**Pay and long-term incentives**

Pay should be competitive to prevent people from leaving the organization to earn more elsewhere.

Long-term incentives can encourage people to couple their careers and personal goals with a long-term commitment to your organization.

For example, if vacation days or other benefits increase over time, people may stay with your organization for longer. Stock options for long-term employees are another common long-term incentive.

**Opportunities for advancement**

If people don't feel that they can advance within an organization, they may seek new positions with different employers.

An organization that wants to retain up-and-coming, talented people has to provide them with genuine opportunities for advancement, or risk losing them.

**Flexible working arrangements**

When working arrangements are inflexible and fixed, the options available to people are circumscribed – sometimes forcing them to choose between staying with an organization and meeting other commitments, such as family obligations.

Allowing people to work more flexible hours, providing adequate leave, or letting people work from home when possible helps retain talent.

**Positive work environment**

People are unlikely to stay in an organization if they're stressed or unhappy. So creating a positive work environment significantly reduces turnover.

Some ways to achieve this are to make sure employees gain satisfaction from their work, feel respected, and are physically comfortable.

It's important for managers to monitor levels of satisfaction among employees so they can forestall problems before people leave an organization.

Regular use of surveys is one way of finding out how satisfied people are with their income, advancement opportunities, working arrangements, and work environments.

**Job Aid**

Four Components of Talent Management

**Purpose:** *Use this job aid to review the components and key activities of talent management.*

| Talent management components | | |
|---|---|---|
| Component | Description | Activities |
| Planning | Planning links talent competencies to your current and future goals, and creates implemen- | Establishing requirements<br>Deciding on a talent focus<br>Defining competencies<br>Establishing criteria |

|  | tation strategies. | Conducting talent audits |
|---|---|---|
| Acquiring | Acquiring talent is about bringing people with desired competencies into your organization. | Attracting<br>Recruiting<br>Selecting<br>Employing |
| Developing | Talent is developed by nurturing and building employees' capabilities. | Career development and training<br>Performance management<br>Coaching and mentoring |
| Retaining | Retaining talent is about preventing employee turnover, which is defined as the percentage of employees who leave an organization voluntarily during a specified period. | To retain talent, you need to provide<br>- competitive pay and long-term incentives<br>- opportunities for advancement<br>- flexible working arrangements<br>- a positive work environment |

Question

Match the activities to the component to which they apply.

**Options:**

A. Providing opportunities for employees to improve their skills

B. Creating a supportive work environment

C. Allowing people to work from a home office when it's more convenient for them

D. Assigning someone to work with talented individuals to help them meet their goals

**Targets:**
1. Developing talent
2. Retaining talent

Answer

*To develop talent, you need to help people develop new skills through training programs, coaching, and mentoring.*

*To retain talent, you need to provide a supportive and positive work environment. Allowing people to work from a home office and recognizing and rewarding talent according to their contributions are examples of how you might do this.*

6. Summary

A complete talent management system should have the following components: planning, acquisition, developing talent, and retaining talent.

Planning involves identifying, defining, and setting criteria for required capabilities, as well as auditing current talent levels.

Acquiring talent requires that you use a wide range of strategies to attract talent and consistent recruitment processes.

Developing talent involves providing opportunities for career development and training, managing employees' performance, and coaching and mentoring.

To retain talent, you need to offer good remuneration, long-term incentives, a flexible and positive work environment, and opportunities for advancement.

# THE MANAGER'S ROLE IN TALENT MANAGEMENT

1. A talent management strategy

Unless managers actively engage in each component of talent management, the process is unlikely to succeed. Senior management needs provide direction and strategic guidance during talent management planning. It's the line and other managers who follow through and implement these initiatives.

As a manager, you're naturally a role model. You shape employee behavior through your actions, words, opinions, and attitudes. What you subtly emphasize or underplay has a powerful influence on what employees do, and how they approach their work.

Managers are also expected to provide guidance and advice, constantly shaping employees' future performance.

Some of the main roles that managers play in implementing talent management initiatives are recruiting and selecting talent effectively, building motivation and commitment, assessing employees, and creating a work environment where talent can thrive.

Question

In what area do you think your main strength lies?

Options:

1. Recruiting and selecting
2. Motivating

3. Assessing
   4. Creating a positive environment

Answer

***Option 1:*** *Knowing how to bring new talent on board and choose the right candidates for the job has a huge impact on how well your organization acquires talent.*

***Option 2:*** *Being able to motivate people and win their commitment is a sign of a true leader, and helps you make the most of the talent in your organization.*

***Option 3:*** *Assessing people and giving them good feedback helps them develop and reach their true potential, so that you foster talent in your organization.*

***Option 4:*** *Managing the workplace environment is a key managerial responsibility, and helps you retain talent in your organization.*

2. Recruitment role

Recruiting and selecting talent effectively requires that you know and define the talent requirements in your area of responsibility. You need to be involved because who you attract and select to work for you will influence the quality of the results you get for your department. Recruiting and selection also affect the number of people you have with the potential to be promoted in the future.

As the manager of a particular department or area of work, you are best placed to define the competencies you need from new personnel – in other words, the talent you require to meet your goals.

These competencies will feed into the job descriptions you use to recruit, interview, and select the best people. You can prioritize these competencies during the recruitment and selection processes.

One of the benefits of recruiting and selecting effectively is that you will hire employees who have the right talent you need to meet your goals.

In turn, you'll have improved performance and productivity.

You can use social networks, your position of authority, and other resources to leverage the recruitment options that will bring you the best results.

As a manager, you are in an ideal position to take note of people who could be recruited for different positions.

It helps to always be thinking about what talent you can recruit and what these people could do in your organization.

Question

What is the role of a manager in implementing the recruitment component of a talent management strategy?

**Options:**

1. Define competencies needed to meet goals in the required area
2. Use competencies to interview for individuals who have the talents needed
3. Watch out for potential talent in the professional circle
4. Create company branding to attract the talent needed
5. Hire employees with the best references

Answer

**Option 1:** *This option is correct. Managers know what talent they need to reach their department's goals. This places them in a key position to define competencies required for each employment gap to be filled effectively.*

**Option 2:** *This option is correct. To select employees with the right potential, you use identified competencies during interviews and create job descriptions that incorporate these competencies.*

**Option 3:** *This option is correct. Your position as a manager provides you with the opportunity and the insight you need to identify talent gaps and who could fill these gaps.*

**Option 4:** *This option is incorrect. Your role is to identify potential talent and define and use competencies to do this. Branding the or-*

*ganization is an executive function.*

**Option 5:** *This option is incorrect. Although this is one aspect of recruiting, it's more important to use competencies to find out who matches your needs.*

### 3. Motivating talent

As a manager, you need to inspire confidence in employees and motivate them to stay in the organization. To do this, you need to be able to guide, coach, and mentor employees, as well as empower them.

Coaching and mentoring enable you to develop people's skills, provide them with new challenges to master, and expand their capabilities.

Coaching and mentoring make people feel supported and cared about. This in turn increases their motivation and commitment.

As a manager, you're well placed to coach and mentor. This is because managers are in an ideal position to observe employees doing their jobs and therefore notice when coaching or mentoring is needed.

Managers are also familiar with the expected work results. So any gaps between what's being done and what's needed to achieve results will alert them to comment on what and how to improve.

As well as guiding, coaching, and mentoring employees, managers need to motivate and engage them. They do this when they empower employees to make their own decisions, build productive teams, commit to the work and their colleagues and clients, create trust and integrity within teams, and provide opportunities for career development.

**Empower**

When people are empowered to make decisions and influence the direction of their work, they become personally engaged with what they do, and identify with their achievements. This is a powerful motivator.

So you need to empower employees to have influence over their work whenever possible. When people feel their opinions are heard and taken seriously, they contribute valuable talents and insights instead of just going along with whatever you, as a manager, suggest.

**Build productive teams**

Building productive teams helps coordinate actions and improve communication. In addition, employees experience bonding and develop trust and respect for one another. When people are part of a group, it helps them have a sense of belonging and purpose. This has a positive impact on morale and motivation.

**Build commitment**

When employees are committed to an organization, they willingly go the extra mile. And good management practices are key in building that commitment. Managers need to communicate business goals and how employees' roles contribute to those goals. Positive feedback is also important.

Finally, managers need to find ways to maximize people's performance and feelings of success by putting them into roles that take advantage of their natural abilities.

**Create trust and integrity**

Central to engaging people is making sure they trust you. There are many behaviors that can help you do this – for example, being straightforward, demonstrating respect, creating transparency, and keeping your promises.

To build trust and integrity, organizations must require that managers act with integrity and keep their commitments. They can also reward leaders and employees who tell the truth.

And managers who treat employees fairly, openly, and honestly build trust – which is an important element in being able to engage and motivate employees.

**Provide opportunities**

Encouraging people to advance their careers engages them. They

# TALENT MANAGEMENT

know they are making a good long-term investment by committing themselves at work. And their work becomes more significant and meaningful, as it's tied to more personal aspirations.

Managers are well placed to give people advice, build their confidence, and guide their ambitions for the future.

When you actively fulfill your motivational role, employees' higher levels of commitment increase productivity and promote success in your area of responsibility.

**Sarah**

"My manager, Frank, has coached me very closely in my dealings with the company's customers. When I started work, I had good formal qualifications, and a fair bit of experience. But I'd never actually had anyone watch me work and tell me how to do better before.

Frank pointed out my strengths and weaknesses, helping me grow and improve. It's a great feeling to be coached in such a supportive way."

**James**

"When my manager created the team for an important project, she worked to make it productive. Under her leadership, we built close and positive relationships, and the team was involved in decisions that would normally be left to managers in other companies. We felt empowered and motivated to do the best work we could."

Question

What can you do to engage your direct reports?

**Options:**
1. Inspire people and encourage them to go the extra mile in their work
2. Encourage employees to make decisions about how they should carry out their work
3. Keep employees busy so that they don't lose their com-

mitment to the job

4. Make sure employees know that you're the leader by establishing strict rules for how to work
5. Bring people together to work on meeting goals effectively
6. Provide opportunities for continuing skill enhancement

Answer

**Option 1:** *This option is correct. Managers need to build employee motivation and commitment to encourage employees to invest their energy, talent, and time.*

**Option 2:** *This option is correct. Empowering employees to make decisions linked to their work helps them to take ownership of the work and provide valuable insights.*

**Option 3:** *This option is incorrect. Motivating employees requires more than simply keeping employees busy.*

**Option 4:** *This option is incorrect. One of the ways to motivate talented employees is to empower them by giving them more responsibility.*

**Option 5:** *This option is correct. Managers can motivate employees by creating productive teams.*

**Option 6:** *This is a correct option. When you provide opportunities for continuing development, you stimulate employees' interests and keep them motivated.*

4. Assessing performance

Performance assessments help managers determine how well employees do their work. Such assessments help protect the integrity of the talent management process because performance is rewarded at the individual level. Consider what would happen if employees were promoted, despite failing or doing poorly in their current jobs at their existing level of responsibility. It would likely destroy the credibility of the promotion system, which is an important factor in talent management.

Assessment incorporates two key ingredients - performance measurement and feedback.

As a manager, you need to clarify what's expected of employees. To do this effectively, expectations should be clear and measurable.

Telling employees to make good sales isn't helpful. However, saying that they need to sell a particular quantity over a specified time period provides a target, or minimum work standard, that employees can aim for.

You need to plan, monitor, and assess results. This means meeting with employees at the start of the year and planning what results they should achieve and how they should achieve them. Then you can regularly check their progress. At the end of the review cycle, you should evaluate their achievements.

Giving feedback involves letting employees know what they're doing well and discussing what they can do to improve. It's essential for improving performance and for developing talent.

It's something that should be done regularly, so that when it comes time for the annual performance appraisal, there are no surprises. Employees already know what you think of their performance because the annual appraisal is really just a summary of the feedback they have been getting from you all along.

You don't need to conduct formal feedback meetings every day. You can give some kind of feedback all the time. For example, you might send a short e-mail or say "excellent work today" when you pass an employee in the hallway.

Suppose you manage a team of laboratory technicians. You notice that one of them is about twice as accurate as everyone else on the team, but takes approximately 30% longer to complete her projects. This reduces the team's overall productivity.

Providing feedback about these observations can help her improve her performance and may even help the rest of the team boost its accuracy.

Question

It's important your employees are clear about what's expected of them. How often should you give them feedback?

Options:

1. Frequently
2. Infrequently
3. When asked to do so

Answer

**Option 1:** *Regular feedback reinforces the credibility of the promotion system because it enables you to give on-site performance measurement and feedback.*

**Option 2:** *Infrequent or irregular feedback has adverse effects on productivity and compromises the credibility of the promotion system. Consider giving your employees frequent or regular feedback.*

**Option 3:** *Providing frequent or regular feedback is essential to meaningful and effective talent management. As such, it is a managerial responsibility.*

5. Creating the right environment

A manager can help talent to thrive by taking an active interest in employee job satisfaction, workplace design, health and safety, job security, work culture, and work-life balance.

**Job satisfaction**

To make jobs meaningful for individual employees, you can offer variety, explain how tasks relate to the whole, or identify how work impacts the lives of others. This in turn increases motivation.

**Workplace design**

As a manager, ensure that offices and other settings for work are ergonomic, pleasant environments. Make the workplaces you manage efficient and comfortable for people to inhabit.

**Health and safety**

Take responsibility for making sure that the people you manage are safe. Take care that potential dangers are removed or controlled, and let people know you care about their health and safety at work.

**Job security**

As a manager, you should demonstrate to people that you aim to provide a stable work environment. Try to keep them employable through skills training. Reassure people you want them to continue with your organization.

**Work culture**

Your leadership can encourage a work culture that supports employees' values, encourages respect and tolerance of differences, creates a dynamic environment, and promotes the dignity of all employees.

**Balance**

By shaping the way people work and providing opportunities for employees to explore personal interests, you help people maintain a balance between their work and personal lives. This is essential to prevent burnout, and to encourage happy and committed employees.

Managers have a pivotal role to play in implementing talent management, which has a significant impact on the productivity and success of an organization. Your contribution to recruitment, motivation, assessment, and the work environment can make all the difference.

**Job Aid**

Implementing Talent Management

**Purpose:** *Use this job aid to help you implement talent management.*

The responsibilities of a manager in implementing talent management are to

- **recruit talent effectively**
    - assess what kind of talent is needed
    - select people with the right talents

- identify potential talent
- **build motivation and commitment**
  - empower employees to make their own decisions
  - provide coaches and mentors
  - create trust
  - build commitment
  - develop employees' careers
- **assess employees**
  - create clear and measurable performance targets for individuals
  - provide regular positive and corrective feedback
- **create a work environment that allows talent to thrive**
  - improve job satisfaction, health and safety, job security, and work-life balance
  - create efficient and pleasant surroundings
  - promote a supportive and tolerant work culture

Question

Which are ways that managers can implement talent management in their organizations?

**Options:**

1. Evaluate employees' performances and let them know where they stand in meeting their goals
2. Create a supportive and efficient setting for people at work
3. Give feedback about poor performance immediately

and forcefully
4. Make sure that the work environment has a television and other distractions to make it more relaxed and creative

Answer

**Option 1:** *This option is correct. When implementing talent management, managers need to assess people's performance and provide feedback on a daily basis. This helps guide and develop talent in their area.*

**Option 2:** *This option is correct. When managing talent, it's important to create and maintain a work environment that allows talent to thrive.*

**Option 3:** *This option is incorrect. This isn't a very effective way to implement talent management. It could demoralize an employee, which is not the aim of a talent management strategy.*

**Option 4:** *This option is incorrect. Creating a comfortable and pleasant environment in which to work helps keep employees happy, but allowing distractions may inhibit creativity rather than promoting it.*

Question

Now you know how to manage talent effectively.

What are the benefits of being able to do this?

**Options:**
1. You're more likely to succeed in winning desired organizational outcomes
2. You can increase your productive output
3. You'll find more enthusiastic employees who are truly invested in their work
4. You're more likely to get the talent you need to achieve the goals for which you are responsible
5. You'll find it easier to cut the costs of employing people
6. You'll know how to promote individuals to manage-

ment positions

Answer

**Option 1:** This option is correct. When managers play an active part in talent management, organizations are more likely to get successful results.

**Option 2:** This is a correct option. Effectively managing talent increases commitment and reduces talent gaps, thereby increasing productivity.

**Option 3:** This option is correct. Effective talent management will help you find more motivated, committed employees.

**Option 4:** This option is correct. When you're involved in recruiting talent, you're more likely to get the talent required to meet goals in your area of responsibility.

**Option 5:** This is an incorrect option. Effective talent management doesn't necessarily affect the costs of employing people.

**Option 6:** This option is incorrect. Talent management isn't just about finding individuals who are suitable for management roles. It's also about recruiting, motivating, and assessing the individuals you work with.

6. Summary

As a manager, you need to be actively involved in recruiting talent, because this impacts the results you can achieve.

You need to motivate employees by coaching and mentoring them. Other ways managers can motivate and engage employees is by empowering them, building productive teams, creating a foundation of trust and integrity, building employee commitment, and providing opportunities for continuing development.

You develop talent through your assessment role, by measuring performance against clear targets and by providing feedback on how well employees are meeting these targets.

**Follow-on Activity**

Improving Your Talent Management

**Purpose:** *Use this follow-on activity to assess your strengths and weaknesses in implementing talent management.*

**Instructions for use:** To use this tool, record your answers to the following questions.

1. How well do you serve as a role model for the people you manage? What could you do to improve?
2. What behavior do you encourage or discourage in others? How does this affect the way talent is developed in your area?
3. Have you defined competencies needed for each job description within your area of responsibility?
4. Do you regularly assign coaches or mentors to individuals based on their needs and potential?
5. Do you encourage people to make their own decisions about their work?
6. Do you regularly assess people for their potential competencies?
7. How frequently do you evaluate people's performances and give them feedback?
8. Do you link individual's tasks to a greater context to provide greater job satisfaction?
9. How often do you train people and reassure them that you want them to continue with the organization?

# TALENT MANAGEMENT: PLANNING

As a manager, ask yourself this: Where is my department or division in relation to developing talent management strategies? Are you aware of your organization's talent needs, and are you supporting these within your area of influence?

Several symptoms may indicate that you need a more systematic approach to talent management:

- a retention risk analysis indicates that your department could lose valuable talent that's difficult to replace, through the retirement or resignation of key employees
- your department is struggling to secure suitable replacements for key employees who leave and it takes too long to replace lost talent
- it's difficult to identify individuals who are ready for promotion – either due to a lack of the necessary competencies or because employees aren't willing to accept new roles
- employees in your department perceive the promotion process as unfair or too random
- protected minority groups aren't represented sufficiently at certain levels within your department or in the organization as a whole, or

- turnover among employees with strong potential is high, or higher than turnover among employees with low or average potential

For talent management to succeed, it must be properly planned. Essentially, talent management involves anticipating the need for human capital – or talent, creating a plan to meet this need, and then implementing the plan.

In this course, you'll learn about the challenges involved in talent management and about the foundations that must be in place for it to succeed.

You'll learn why it's important to determine talent needs, and which factors can affect these needs.

And you'll learn how to create an effective talent management plan for addressing the needs you identify.

**Talent Management Planning**

1. Challenges of Managing Talent
2. Determining Your Talent Needs
3. Developing a Talent Management Plan

# CHALLENGES OF MANAGING TALENT

**1. Recognizing talent management challenges**

To succeed, an organization has to have the talent to meet its needs. But as a manager, can you identify and attract the right people to meet these needs? Can you keep these people with your organization over the long term? And will those same people meet your organization's needs in the future? Before starting to address your organization's talent needs, you need to be aware of the challenges you'll face.

If you question the importance of talent management, you should be aware that top talent is a valuable resource that can give an organization a competitive edge. Talented people can make a big difference in an organization's performance.

Some of the talent management challenges you'll face will be finding people who are the right fit, retaining talent, and forecasting the future talent needs of your organization.

**Finding the right fit**

Finding the right fit refers to matching people's talents to roles in which they can be fully utilized and further developed.

It's an important concern because you can prevent turnover by matching people's interests and abilities to the right role.

**Retaining talent**

Recruiting and training new talent is expensive and time-consuming. So it's important to prevent your organization from losing talented employees it's already secured, trained, and developed.

**Forecasting future talent needs**

You need to forecast future needs so you can determine the talent that must be hired or developed to support these needs. If you fail to do this, a talent shortfall will occur – it's too late to start securing talent once a need has appeared.

Finding the right fit involves attracting people with needed talents and ensuring they're appointed to roles in which their talents can be best used.

Take the example of Andrew, a software programmer who was hired because of his coding expertise. Based on his good performance as a programmer, his manager decided to promote him to the position of team leader. Unfortunately, Andrew lacks the skills needed to manage other employees effectively.

In this case, Andrew isn't the right fit for the team leadership position. To find the right fit, his manager should have better determined which role suited his talents.

To help them find the right fit, companies need to attract the right talent from across the pool of available employees. One of the challenges in doing this is successfully attracting talent from different generations.

**Attracting talent from different generations**

Members of different generations – including the so-called Generation X, baby boomers, and Generation Y – have different work values, expectations, and priorities. For example, older employees may prioritize job security, whereas younger employees often prioritize opportunities for career development. It's a challenge for companies to appeal to multiple generations because of the employees' diverse values and needs.

A significant challenge for companies is retaining talent. You've no doubt invested time and resources developing the talent of employees with high potential. If those employees leave before they've had the opportunity to apply that talent, another company will reap the rewards of your investment.

# TALENT MANAGEMENT

Betty, the HR manager of a publishing house, is concerned about the fact that many staff members with high potential stay at the company just long enough to gain valuable experience and development opportunities. They then move to other positions with other companies.

Betty should realize that talented employees are very hard to keep in today's competitive environment. Her company is currently serving as a training ground for its competitors. If this issue isn't addressed, it's likely the company will face serious talent shortages.

Another example of the challenge of talent retention is the corporate talent gap created by Generation Xers leaving corporate careers. Often businesses have invested significantly in these talented individuals and expect them to fill leadership positions.

Companies also need to appeal to – and try to retain – talented individuals from the near-retirement or retired baby boomers and from the younger Generation Y. That way they'll have the largest possible pool of talent to choose from.

If managers fail to forecast future talent needs, they set their organizations up for future talent shortages.

**Unito Games**

Unito Games failed to predict a surge in its growth when hiring entry-level recruits during the annual college graduation period. As a result, it faced a talent shortage. After the next annual graduation, it hires enough recruits to compensate for its past oversight, and to meet anticipated future needs. However, this puts sudden strain on the company in terms of training – because it's retroactively catching up with its talent needs.

**Diallonic**

After receiving a huge contract, Diallonic promoted several of its top software developers to management positions. This left the company short of developers, a situation which was exacerbated when a few of the remaining developers left because they were overworked. As a result, the company's in an uncomfortable position – it needs to either try to attract a large number of talented developers, or fast track recent graduates through training, which requires a lot of resources.

For both companies, failing to forecast future needs had a knock-on effect, where talent supply lagged behind demand.

For Unito Games, a lack of forecasting meant the company lacked talent until the next graduate hiring opportunity arose. It hired to fill a past gap, but any slowing of business would leave the organization overstaffed.

In Diallonic's case, the company promoted talent internally. This left it with a talent shortage in certain areas.

Question

During its peak season, an expanding retailer has to cope with the unexpected departures of several store managers. The company quickly promotes floor managers to fill the gaps. Several are unable to cope with the pressure and resign. There is also a talent shortage on the shop floors.

Which talent management challenges is the retailer facing?

**Options:**

1. Matching the talents of staff to the roles that best suit them
2. Trying to anticipate and cater for future needs
3. Preventing an oversupply of talent
4. Finding employees who can cope with extra work while the retailer decides what to do

Answer

**Option 1:** *This option is correct. The company failed to find the right fit with the new managers it promoted, and as a result, some of these managers left.*

**Option 2:** *This is a correct option. The company didn't have suitably prepared staff in place to assume the store management positions, or to replace the floor managers who were promoted.*

*Option 3:* This is an incorrect option. The company is facing a shortage of talent rather than an oversupply.

*Option 4:* This option is incorrect. Although this would be a stop-gap solution, putting increased pressure on reliable employees may make them consider leaving.

Question

A financial consulting company has a good graduate recruitment program that has it taking in and developing the most promising young employees in the financial sector. The company has an increasing problem that many of these employees leave once the training is complete, but before they can make a talent contribution to the company.

Which talent management problem is this company facing?

**Options:**
1. A failure to meet future talent needs
2. A problem finding new employees that are a good fit with the organization
3. A surplus of talent
4. A problem with talent retention and wasted development efforts

Answer

*Option 1:* This option is incorrect. The company takes in sufficient talent to cater for talent needs, but has a problem retaining them.

*Option 2:* This is an incorrect option. The company has a sizeable intake of new employees, but has trouble retaining them.

*Option 3:* This option is incorrect. The company is suffering a talent shortage due to a lack of talent retention.

*Option 4:* This is the correct option. The loss of recently developed high potential staff is a talent retention problem.

2. Foundations of talent management

Talent management is a complex process. For it to succeed, certain organizational foundations should be in place. These include executive commitment, structured processes, and measures and metrics.

Executive commitment is vital to the success of a talent management initiative. Without it, an initiative won't gain the required resources or support. There are different levels of commitment. Executives could provide zero commitment, express some support, offer support and presence, or provide total commitment.

**Zero commitment**

When executives offer zero commitment, they offer no support and won't even consider talent management plans. The only positive point is that you won't waste any time working on a talent management plan that will be ignored.

**Express support**

Executives may express support verbally but fail to back this up in any way. But without input and continued resource allocation, nobody will take talent management seriously.

**Support and presence**

Executives may provide verbal support and presence, allocating resources but not taking an active role in talent management. In this case, executives limit their input to a consulting level.

Without more active involvement by executives, a talent management initiative is unlikely to be perceived as valuable. This diminishes others' support for it.

**Total commitment**

Total commitment is the best-case scenario. This is where executives view talent management as aligned to company goals and to their personal success. They'll actively champion a talent management initiative and state that they expect others' support.

Total commitment from executives gives a talent management initiative the best chance of success. Without it, you may get executive support and passive input, but other projects will always be perceived as more valuable.

As well as executive support, there must be well-structured processes in place for implementing talent management. Creating these processes typically requires a combination of business design, management shifting, and careful consultation.

When designing a talent management process, you should ask questions like these:

- Which talent choices will you make?
- What information must be gathered to support choices, and how will it be gathered?
- What techniques will you use to get that information?
- How must the information be organized to inform the choices you make?

Talent management processes mustn't be sound only on paper. To succeed, they have to be embedded in the organization and have the necessary executive support.

Talent management plans fall flat if their results are perceived as having minimal business value. To demonstrate the value of talent management to stakeholders like executives, you need to determine appropriate measures and metrics. Using these, you can demonstrate value based on employees' experience of talent management, its results, and its impact on the organization.

**Employees' experience**

One way to quantify the value of a talent management program is to measure employees' experience of it. For example, is it meeting people's expectations? How easy is it to follow? And how do those involved in or affected by it rate its quality? It's important to gather this information to evaluate any training, and it lays the groundwork for further measurements.

For example, if a candidate who completes a management training program finds it to be good for acquiring skills but often difficult to follow, it shows you that this area needs to be tweaked.

**Results**

The results of a talent management program can be measured against the program's specified objective. Did it deliver what you wanted? If it didn't, why?

For example, if you were running a course for prospective candidates for management positions, you could ask yourself how many of them completed the course, or how many of them were ready for promotion. If there was a high rate of drop outs, you'd need to discover where the problem lay.

**Impact**

You should quantify the overall impact of a talent management program on your organization. For example, it may be reflected in the number of staff promoted within the organization, or in less immediate business improvements.

Take the example of a talent management program at a bank which aims to have clerks progress up the corporate ladder to management positions. After a year, more than half of all middle and lower management positions are filled by staff who started in junior roles. This means the plan had a positive impact.

Question

Remember Betty? She decides to implement a talent management program to develop the capabilities of a group of employees with high potential and to retain talented employees.

What elements should be in place for Betty's talent management initiative to be successful?

**Options:**

1. Sound structured talent management processes that are embedded in the organization
2. External advertising campaigns that could attract some of the departed employees back to the company in order to find out what they learned while working at other organizations
3. Full support from executives who believe in the talent management plan, are prepared to allocate resources

to her, and who will actively campaign for it at board meetings and in company memos
4. Methods that allow her to measure the impact of the talent management initiative on the organization
5. A system to get the input of graduates to determine what would draw them to her company

Answer

***Option 1:*** *This option is correct. Every talent management plan needs a well-structured process to succeed, otherwise the disparate elements won't work together and the plan won't yield results.*

***Option 2:*** *This option is incorrect. Betty should collect sufficient information in order to plan thoroughly, but it would be far better to retain current staff than to try tempt former employees to return.*

***Option 3:*** *This is a correct option. If Betty can get total executive commitment, she'll know management and other employees will regard her plan as a priority.*

***Option 4:*** *This option is correct. Measuring the results and impact of the plan should allow her to determine whether it's running efficiently, and demonstrate its value to executives and managers.*

***Option 5:*** *This is an incorrect option. While feedback from graduates may be useful for future initiatives, it'll have no impact on her current talent management program.*

## 3. Summary

Before you start to plan a talent management program, you must recognize the challenges and organizational foundations you'll be dealing with. The challenges include finding the right fit for talent within the organization, reducing staff turnover and retaining talent, and forecasting future talent needs.

The foundations of a good talent management plan include total executive commitment, a well-structured process for the plan, and measures and metrics to test its efficacy.

# DETERMINING YOUR TALENT NEEDS

1. Determining talent needs

Before you can recruit, develop, and retain talented people for your organization, you must determine what type of talent your organization needs, and what talent it already has. This will tell you what talent must still be acquired or developed.

The process of determining the organization's talent needs has three main benefits. It gives you a more realistic sense of your department's bench strength. You'll be more successful in fulfilling organizational objectives related to talent management. And you'll be more proactive in developing talent to meet your company's future needs.

**Sense of bench strength**

The process of determining talent needs will give you a realistic idea of the number and capabilities of existing employees. This will result in your knowing who's adequately prepared to fill available leadership and other positions within your department and organization. You'll also know whether you need to develop more talent so you can maintain the productivity of your department if someone leaves.

**Successful in fulfilling objectives**

To determine what your talent needs are, you compare all existing talent against what your organization needs in order to meet its goals. This is crucial because it helps ensure that you align your efforts to recruit, develop, and retain talent with the overall objectives of the company.

## Proactive in developing talent

Knowing your talent needs enables you to be more proactive when it comes to acquiring and developing the people you need for your company to be successful in the future. Being aware of these talent needs means you'll be clear about the competencies that are required, and this will guide you in hiring, selecting, developing, and retaining employees that are most appropriate for the positions you need to fill.

Question

What are the benefits of determining your organization's talent needs?

**Options:**

1. You'll have a better idea of how many employees are currently equipped to fill important positions that become available
2. You'll know how best to go about securing the talent your organization needs
3. You'll be able to secure full executive commitment for a talent management initiative
4. You'll know how best to focus talent management activities
5. You'll be better able to align talent management activities with your company's objectives

Answer

*Option 1: This option is correct. The process of determining talent needs includes determining what talent is already available. It will give you a realistic idea of the number and competencies of employees available to fill important positions that become vacant.*

*Option 2: This is an incorrect option. The process of determining your organization's talent needs doesn't tell you how best to address those needs – only what the needs are.*

*Option 3: This option is incorrect. Simply identifying what your organization needs won't guarantee that executives view a talent* management initiative as having sufficient business value.

**Option 4**: This is a correct option. Once you know your organization's talent needs, you can focus talent management activities on meeting these needs.

**Option 5**: This option is correct. Determining your organization's talent needs involves assessing what talent is required to support the organization's objectives. It helps ensure that you align talent management activities with these overall objectives.

Acquiring the most suitable talent to meet the needs of your organization requires a methodical approach – and this is why planning is important. The aim of planning is to define a systematic process for acquiring the talent that's needed, given the constraints of market forces and the available labor supply.

Typically, the HR Department, CEO, and other senior leaders will decide what the main focus of an organization's talent management process should be.

For instance, will the focus be purely on individuals who have the greatest potential? If so, the concept of "greatest potential" needs to be defined so it's clearly understood.

Does it refer to individuals who can move into leadership roles within two years, regardless of their current positions? Or to those counted as overachievers? Or perhaps to individuals who consistently improve working practices?

Alternatively, the focus could be on all employees that have potential talent. The talent management process would then center around developing staff with high potential at all levels within an organization.

Whatever focus the organization decides on, it should establish what competencies and abilities make up the talents you've identified as talents you need – and how they can be assessed, measured, and developed.

Organizations should also identify criteria for measuring both the existing and potential capabilities of individuals. This can be in the form of competencies specific to the organization, or common predictors of potential, such as emotional intelligence.

As a manager, you're responsible for managing talent in your department – and you can't manage talent if you don't assess your own particular talent needs first.

There are five key factors you need to be aware of that influence talent needs:

- how talent is defined within the organization
- what the current level of talent is within the organization
- any identified replacement needs
- the strategic requirements of the company, and
- current or anticipated changes in skills and competencies within the company

Question

Why should managers at all levels be knowledgeable about their organization's talent management process?

**Options:**

1. So they can implement the process effectively in their areas of responsibility
2. So they can assist in improving HR policies and guidelines
3. So they can be more effective in identifying the talent needs of other company departments

Answer

Managers need to be aware of their organization's talent management process because they have the duty of implementing it in their specific areas. They'll be responsible for assessing their particular talent needs and for using criteria defined at the organizational level to assess competencies.

## 2. Factors affecting talent needs

How talent is defined is an important factor. Knowing what talent you're looking for will affect how you recruit, develop, promote, and reward employees.

To define talent effectively, you can use a competency model. This lists the competencies individuals should possess to be considered suitable for key positions.

The model is usually developed at an organizational level, but managers can contribute to its development.

Once an organization knows what talents it's looking for, it should assess whether current employees possess them.

Sometimes companies don't realize what talent already exists in-house. Because this affects talent needs, it's useful to do a talent audit before you start sourcing talent from outside the company.

A talent audit helps you review and identify possible talent gaps within your company. To know which talents to review and how employees should be measured during the audit, you should rely on information from your competency model.

Tyrone is a senior manager for a magazine publisher that has recently decided to launch a new magazine. The company now needs to acquire talent – either internally or externally – to fill key positions that will contribute to the creation of the new publication.

The company has developed a competency model that outlines the talents that will be required for this new venture.

Tyrone checks the availability of existing in-house talent against the competency model created.

He then conducts a talent audit and asks himself three questions:

- What are my toughest departmental challenges?
- Do I currently have enough talent in my department?
- What could happen three years from now that may affect the number and type of staff required?

**Departmental challenges?**

The new publication venture presents Tyrone and his department with various challenges.

Tyrone has to ensure that the new publication meets readers' interest; the publication has to meet the high editorial standards of the company; sales of the new publication have to meet or exceed sales targets; and interesting and profitable advertising opportunities for large advertising spenders have to be created.

**Enough talent?**

Tyrone's talent audit reveals that there's not enough talent available in-house to make the new venture a success. He therefore has to ensure that new talent is recruited for areas where it's lacking.

**Three years from now?**

In the long run, the company is following new developments in the field of social media and is looking at ways to leverage its potential to increase profit and reader involvement.

To meet these long-term goals, the company's looking at various advertisement opportunities and hosting marketing campaigns. This means that the company will need additional talent for this area in the near future.

A third factor to consider is replacement needs, which arise as employees leave your organization or department. For example, employees may retire, resign, or be transferred to other office locations or departments.

This can leave either sudden gaps in talent that need to be filled – in the case of sudden staff illness – or gaps that can be planned for – such as eventual employee retirement. So it's critical that your replacement planning focuses on both the current and future needs of the organization – both your short-term and long-term needs.

The talent management process is crucial in the replacement of this lost talent, because it's used to effectively recruit and prepare new talent.

In replacement planning, identifying backups for the short and long term is crucial and can be done by using a simple chart. Map out your department structure, listing the key employees who report to you and their positions. Identify individuals from within your company who'd be ideal backups should you and other key employees have to be replaced. Then assign the number "1" to the backups who are best suited to fill the relevant roles.

Next you assess the readiness of each backup. Can the individual move into the role immediately? If this is the case, mark the person you've identified as "R" – meaning "Ready." If not, estimate and record the length of time needed to develop the individual's skills adequately and, next to the "R", add the number of days, weeks, or months.

Unexpectedly, Tyrone's most experienced staff member, Wendy, informs him that she's decided to resign and will be leaving at the end of the month.

Tyrone now needs to find someone who has the requisite talents to fill Wendy's role. He reviews his competency model and conducts a talent audit.

He realizes that Wendy's resignation creates a significant talent gap, as she was in charge of the magazine's design and layout department. Of everyone there, she has the most experience and technical know-how.

Question

A company produces camping gear and men's leisure wear. Beverly manages the team that designs the men's leisure wear. After looking into what clients want and the latest fashion trends, the company decides to expand by introducing a line of women's leisure wear, for which Beverly will be responsible. Also, Beverly has recently been informed that one of her primary designers is pregnant and will be taking maternity leave in six months' time.

How are Beverly's talent needs affected by the factors described in this scenario?

**Options:**

# TALENT MANAGEMENT

1. The inclusion of the line of women's leisure wear will require the current talents of Beverly's employees to be reviewed
2. The expansion to include a new line of clothing will mean that Beverly has to create a talent management plan
3. The fact that one of her team members will be taking maternity leave will create a temporary replacement need
4. The team member taking maternity leave will result in Beverly being forced to take over her responsibilities
5. The abilities required of employees to create women's leisure wear will need to be ascertained

Answer

**Option 1:** *This is a correct option. Beverly will have to review the competency model and conduct a talent audit to determine what the current level of talent is, and whether additional talent is required to produce the women's leisure wear line.*

**Option 2:** *This option is incorrect. Talent management plans are developed by the HR department, CEO, and senior leaders, and then provided to managers to implement in their specific departments.*

**Option 3:** *This option is correct. When the team member goes on maternity leave, this will create a talent gap that needs to be filled. Beverly therefore needs to plan an appropriate backup for this key employee.*

**Option 4:** *This option is incorrect. Beverly will have to create a replacement plan identifying more than one backup for the key employee.*

**Option 5:** *This option is correct. The company will have to create a competency model based on the talents required to produce women's leisure wear. Beverly can contribute towards creating this model.*

Talent management plans should be closely aligned with an organization's strategic goals and vision. So managers should ensure they always know what their organization's short-term and long-term strategies are. It's especially important they know of any plans for the organization's growth – which can be affected by shifts in products and services, acquisitions, mergers, and expansion. This can have significant effects on talent requirements, and may make it necessary to re-assign various employees to different functions.

This is evident in Beverly's situation. Her company's decision to expand into an additional market by introducing a new line of women's leisure wear will affect the company's talent requirements.

The expansion will require new talent, and a greater workforce may be required – especially since one of Beverly's key personnel will be on maternity leave.

By being aware of her company's strategies, Beverly can identify the necessary talent requirements and prepare adequately for the changes that'll take place.

When Beverly's company first decided to expand into women's leisure wear, it had to conduct market research. The company therefore recruited individuals with specific market research expertise. And once it had decided on the direction in which to expand, it was necessary to put together a marketing team to market the new venture. This required identifying individuals with the competencies necessary to market products.

The final factor affecting talent needs is changes in skills and competencies. This is brought about by constant technological progression, market changes, and the development of new products or improvements to existing ones.

These factors often create a need for skills and competencies beyond those that already exist in an organization.

In Tyrone's situation, for instance, a new publication will be directed at a different market. In turn, this creates a need for new talent.

**Job Aid**

TALENT MANAGEMENT

Factors to Consider

**Purpose:** *Use this job aid to review the factors you should consider when determining the talent needs for your department.*

**How talent is defined**
- What does my organization define as "talent"?
- What competencies can I identify in my organization's competency model?
- What talents are critical to my department?
- What criteria will I use to assess, measure, and develop necessary competencies?

**The current level of talent in my department**
- What talents already exist in my department?
- What talent gaps have been identified by my talent audit?
- What are my most difficult departmental challenges?
- Do I have enough talent – now and in the future – to address departmental challenges?
- What may happen in the future that will affect the number and type of employees in my department?

**Replacement needs**
- Who are the key employees I identified in my replacement plan?
- Who are the backups I identified in my replacement plan?
- What talent gaps may retirement, resignation, illness, or vacation create?

**Strategic needs of my organization**
- What are the strategic needs of my organization?
- Is my organization considering a shift in product or service, or an acquisition or merger?

**Changes in skills and competencies**

- What skills or competencies may change in my department?
- What additional skills and competencies may be necessary in my department?
- What changes in my organization may create a need for skills and competencies to change?

This is also the case in Beverly's situation. Her company wants to remain competitive and expand into another market. Its decision to include women's leisure wear in addition to the camping gear and men's leisure wear that it already produces means that employee talents have to be reviewed. The abilities that the new venture will require of employees will also need to be reviewed.

Question

The retailer Beverly works for achieves huge success through its expansion into women's leisure wear. Because of this success, the company decides to incorporate children's wear as well, and asks Beverly to take this responsibility on. She's excited despite the fact that her primary designer is on maternity leave, and that three other members of her team have also been lost due to retirement and sudden illness.

How are Beverly's talent needs affected by the decision to include another line of clothing?

**Options:**

1. The new line of children's wear may require staff to be split between designing men's, women's, and children's wear
2. The fact that the department has less employees will require Beverly to shorten her primary designer's maternity leave
3. The expansion to include children's wear could create a need for additional competencies above those that already exist
4. The company's expansion will require Beverly to as-

sess the competency needs of the department that ships the camping gear

Answer

**Option 1:** *This is a correct option. A change like this one in the organization's strategic direction creates new talent needs. It may mean that new employees must be hired or that existing employees must be assigned new functions.*

**Option 2:** *This option is incorrect. Beverly can't shorten the maternity leave to which an employee is entitled, and she can't prevent other replacement needs from occurring. What she can do is plan appropriately for the replacement needs it's possible to anticipate.*

**Option 3:** *This is a correct option. The creation and development of new products, or improvements of existing ones, changes the skills and competencies required.*

**Option 4:** *This is an incorrect option. Beverly should be concerned with the competencies required in her specific department, rather than with those needed in other departments.*

3. Summary

To plan talent management effectively, you have to determine your organization's talent needs.

Factors that affect talent needs include how talent is defined within the organization, the current level of talent within the organization, what replacement needs exist, the organization's strategic requirements, and changes in required skills and competencies.

**Follow-on Activity**

Your Organization's Factors

**Purpose:** *Use this follow-on activity to assess how certain factors in your organization affect your talent management needs.*

**Instructions for use:** To use this tool, consider how each of the following factors in your organization affects your talent needs.

- How do you define talent?
- What is your organization's current level of talent?

- What are your organization's replacement needs?
- What are your organization's strategic needs?
- Will you have to change the skills and competencies within your organization?

# DEVELOPING A TALENT MANAGEMENT PLAN

## 1. Talent management plan components

Once you've determined your talent needs, you're ready to start planning. A good talent management plan should be like a map, showing how you'll attract people to the organization and how you'll develop their talents in line with the organization's objectives.

Every plan will differ depending on the needs of the organization. A plan may be concerned with recruiting, developing, or retaining talent, or a combination of the three. However, each plan should involve three components – a focus, objectives, and actions to meet those objectives.

**Focus**

The focus aims to put all the elements into context – the cause of the talent management problem, the direction the plan will go in, and which people will be targeted by it.

**Objectives**

The objectives are the aims of the plan – they address the problems identified through analysis and in the focus. These should be aligned to the organization's strategies and communicated to all employees.

**Actions**

The actions are the steps you outline for achieving the objectives you've set, given the focus you've identified.

## 2. Focus

The focus of a talent management plan establishes the foundation on which the other plan components can be built. To determine an appropriate focus, you should identify the organization's problems and priorities, determine the human component that the plan will target, and gather further information. Talent management involves helping employees excel in line with company goals, so the focus of the plan should be on how this can be achieved.

To establish an appropriate focus, you should also review your organization's priorities. This will help you identify the talent needed to back up the organization's key strategies.

For example, an organization's priorities may make it clear that it requires a sufficient talent pool to supply a greater number of managers in the near future. In this case, a talent management plan should focus on identifying and developing employees with management potential.

Once you've identified the organization's key strategies, you need to determine the target of your talent management plan. It could be to manage the talent of a small group of key individuals, or to build the skills and competencies of all employees in the organization.

### Key individuals

If the success of a business depends on a small group of high-potential individuals, a talent management plan may be targeted at attracting, developing, and retaining only these individuals.

For example, a law firm may require a few key skilled partners after some older partners retire. It may then target a small group of top-performing advocates with the potential to become partners.

### All employees

A company may focus its talent management planning on all its employees, rather than concentrating on only certain individuals. This reflects a belief that the sum of the talent of an entire organization is greater than its parts. It involves trying to create an environment that boosts performance as a whole.

For example, an airline company needs to maintain a blanket standard of excellent customer service. So it may focus talent management efforts on all its employees – by implementing a training program, for instance.

After you've identified the employees your plan will be targeted at, you might want to conduct an employee survey to discover how motivated your employees are. The results of this survey could affect the intended focus of your talent management plan.

Take the example of an airline company that identifies all its employees as the target for a talent management plan. Responses to a questionnaire reveal that employees in several departments aren't confident about the growth potential of their roles in the organization, and feel they would need to change jobs if they wanted to progress.

Because such a negative outlook could affect performance, changes should be made even if there was initially no intent to develop employees' talents. If there were plans to identify and fast-track talent from certain areas, this finding would be especially problematic.

At this point in the process, you should ask yourself various questions. The answers to these should help determine the target and focus of your plan. For example, if your company is going through a merger, you may want to focus on attracting new talent or on aligning existing talent with the organization's new goals.

As well as assessing your own plans, it's a good idea to chat with business colleagues. By discussing the plan with others, you can judge their interest, get their support, and create allies to help with the process.

If you're not speaking to people from the HR Department, it's best to use a business approach when demonstrating the potential of your plan.

In a decentralized company, however, you should approach HR people first. You do so because talent management forms a large part of their duties, and they may be able to point you in the direction of other people you should interact with.

When discussing your plan with others, there are certain aspects of it you should cover:

- the talent management problem
- the causes of the problem
- the way in which a talent management plan could provide a solution, and
- the way you want to implement a talent management improvement

In a talent management plan, it's always a good idea to start on a relatively small scale, by focusing on a problem of a manageable size. For example, you may choose to focus on identifying employees suitable for developing into managers in a single department, instead of across all departments.

Trying to facilitate change on a massive level is far riskier, because it requires a much larger investment of resources and research. It's also less likely to yield immediate, positive results.

By successfully implementing a plan with a more manageable scope, you'll gain increased support – and this can be the starting point for larger talent management plans.

Question

Take the example of a small accounting firm in which a few of the key partners are nearing retirement.

Which are considerations when deciding who and what to focus on in a talent management plan?

**Options:**

1. An identified need to replace partners who retire

2. The firm's primary goals
3. How competitors have handled similar issues and the results of their solutions
4. How motivated the current workforce is
5. Departing partners' opinions on who should replace them

Answer

**Option 1:** *This option is correct. Every talent management plan should focus directly on an organization's talent needs. Talent management involves helping employees excel in line with company goals, so the focus of the plan should be on how this can be achieved.*

**Option 2:** *This is a correct option. Talent management plans should always align to the primary goals of an organization, or the results won't serve the talent needs of the company.*

**Option 3:** *This option is incorrect. Every talent management plan should be determined based on the carefully researched needs of an organization. Even if your research includes other organizations' plans, your own organization's talent needs should be the focus.*

**Option 4:** *This option is correct. An employee survey is a good way to discover how receptive staff would be to a talent management initiative, and if there are any additional motivational challenges you must overcome.*

**Option 5:** *This is an incorrect option. A talent management plan should concentrate foremost on the organization's talent needs. Although you may consult departing employees as part of your research, they'll have no part in setting objectives or executing the plan.*

3. Objectives

The priorities you set while determining the focus of your plan can help you set the plan's objectives, as long as they're in line with the company's priorities. Imagine a retailer that prides itself on its ability to nurture junior employees through the company. It identifies the recruitment of technically skilled people as a priority. Following on from that, the company's objectives would be to attract, recruit, and retain technical staff.

It's important to communicate the objectives you identify to all managers in your organization. This is to ensure that all managers work in alignment to support the objectives, and understand their associated responsibilities.

The process of defining objectives also gives you the opportunity to address any problems you've identified in the talent management focus. You may set your objectives in terms of development and training or the recruitment and retention of employees, or you could determine them in response to the results of an employee survey.

For example, you might determine the talents of various groups of employees, and decide how to close the gap between your present talent resources and your future talent needs. You could do this through a training program.

To close a talent gap or solve a talent-related problem, you may need to formulate objectives to promote internal talent, hire external talent, or retain existing talent in your organization.

**Promote internal talent**

Identifying staff with the potential for advancement and the capabilities to fill key positions enables you to promote internal talent.

Consider a firm with a lead accountant who's nearing retirement. It may be possible to groom several mid-level employees so that one of them can replace the lead accountant who leaves. Developing internal talent not only ensures there are no skill gaps in the future, but also generates job satisfaction by offering internal opportunities for advancement. It's also less expensive to train someone who knows the company than to train someone who's unfamiliar with the work.

**Hire external talent**

If the internal talent pool isn't sufficient, it may be necessary to hire external talent to close talent gaps.

For example, if a senior manager was nearing retirement, you would need to draft an accurate job description and evaluate all applicants for the position, keeping in mind the objectives of the company.

**Retain existing talent**

Retaining existing talent in a competitive marketplace can help prevent your organization from experiencing a talent shortage. So the objective of a talent management plan may be to retain a group of employees with key skills.

Examples of tools for doing this include financial and other rewards, and including more of the work the employees enjoy in their day-to-day tasks. So your organization could offer a junior employee who's performing to the satisfaction of everyone more responsibility, and accompany it with an increase in salary or benefits. Or your organization may want to consider telecommuting options for a talented employee who's just returned from maternity leave but has expressed an interest in working from home, for example.

Other talent management objectives could include forming partnerships with business graduate schools or corporate recruiters, or implementing formal development programs.

These avenues could provide a readily available talent pool if your organization isn't in a position to recruit new talent frequently.

The objectives you set should be clear and measurable. They should also be realistic and achievable.

Say a car dealership has a plan in place to train 50% of sales employees for supervisor roles per year. The resources required to implement the plan are four times the amount available, but overzealous managers push the plan through, hoping to cut corners to get desired results. Needless to say, the plan fails, and the overall quality of training is poor.

Question

Which objectives are appropriate for a talent management plan?

**Options:**

1. Develop the management skills of promising mid-level employees to provide a pool of at least five potential managers within a year
2. Double sales figures by hiring 50% more entry-level sales people
3. Reduce staff turnover in the Research and Development Department by 40% within two years
4. Improve the retention of employees with key skills

Answer

*Option 1:* This option is correct. This objective is clear and realistic, and its results are measurable.

*Option 2:* This option is incorrect. Although the results of this objective are easily measurable, the objective seems unrealistic. It would need to be backed up by solid research for it to be worth pursuing.

*Option 3:* This is a correct option. This is an easily measurable and realistic objective.

*Option 4:* This is an incorrect option. This objective is too vague. It isn't measurable because it doesn't specify the extent to which retention should be improved or identify which employees – or which key skills – should be targeted.

## 4. Actions

The actions you list describe how your objectives will be met – exactly how you'll discover, attract, and recruit talent, or develop existing talent to meet the organization's needs. When establishing these actions, you should keep the focus of your talent management plan in mind at all times.

For example, an international chain of travel agents is facing high turnover of key managers and executives, and has an inadequate supply of potential successors.

So the focus of the company's talent management plan must be on developing potential leaders and retaining existing top managers.

Appropriate objectives for the plan would relate to developing employees for leadership positions and retaining key management and executive employees. These objectives would then determine the types of actions that the company could take.

**Developing employees for leadership**

An example of an action for achieving the objective of developing employees for leadership positions is implementing a leadership development program to groom selected employees for management positions.

**Retaining key employees**

Examples of actions for achieving the objective of retaining key employees are instituting a program to reward performance, and providing these employees with appropriate development opportunities.

When you describe the actions required to meet your objectives, you need to specify the necessary steps to do so, set milestone dates, and provide measurable target outcomes.

In the case of the leadership development program, all the steps of the program would be listed, from the introduction to the debriefing. This would take place within a structured framework, and you could then measure the results against the targets you've specified.

The executive retention program would consist of all the actual steps of the plan, from the initial assessment to the final feedback sessions. These events would take place on a strict timeline and feedback would be gathered from participants to rate their motivation and projected future with the company.

It's also common to target actions to a single high-potential employee. Developing individual talent is useful for small companies. It can also pay off for larger companies, especially if the person targeted has required expertise in a particular field.

Say a middle manager has been identified as having the potential to progress to executive level, but also has talents in the areas of HR management and portfolio management.

A talent management plan for this individual would need to be custom created, to develop the manager's diverse talents in the direction that would most benefit both the manager and the company.

You should review every talent management plan frequently, so that you can track all the commitments you made. This will allow you to rectify mistakes, and re-align the focus of the plan if necessary.

**Job Aid**

Talent Management Plan Components

**Purpose:** *Use this job aid to review the components of an effective talent management plan.*

**Focus**

The focus of a talent management plan includes the specific talent management problem or challenge to be addressed, and which people the plan should target. To define an appropriate focus, you should conduct research and gather input from other managers. You may also consider using a survey to gauge the motivation of existing employees.

In an engineering company, for example, you may define the focus of a talent management program as being to overcome a shortage of entry-level engineers, and therefore target the plan at engineering graduates, who may be recruited to fill available positions.

**Objectives**

The objectives for a talent management plan specify its goals. These should be clear, measurable, and achievable. The objectives must also align with the organization's overall needs and strategic objectives.

An example of an objective for the engineering company's talent management plan is "to recruit a minimum of ten new entry-level engineers by the end of the year."

**Actions**

Actions are scheduled steps that must be taken to meet the specified objectives. For each action, you should include milestone dates and provide target outcomes.

Actions you might specify to support the objective of recruiting entry-level engineers, for example, are devising job descriptions for the available positions, advertising the positions, sending recruiting agents to graduate schools, and carefully planning the steps involved in the entire interviewing and hiring process. The target outcome is the hiring of an appropriate number of new recruits.

Question

Match the examples to the corresponding components of a talent management plan.

**Options:**

    A.    The plan targets top performers with management potential

    B.    Develop top performers in the organization to produce a minimum of five candidates for managerial positions within a year

    C.    Implement a mentoring program in which existing managers train employees with high leadership potential starting June 1, and assess the results every three months for a year

**Targets:**

    1. Focus

    2. Objective

    3. Actions

Answer

*The focus should identify the employees targeted by the plan – in this example, top performers with management potential.*

*The objective of a plan should state what needs to be accomplished to address a talent management problem. It should be specific, measurable, and achievable. For example, you can determine whether five suitable candidates for management positions are available after a year.*

*The actions outlined in a plan are the practical steps needed to achieve the objectives. Implementing a mentoring program is an example. Actions should be scheduled and have measurable outcomes.*

5. Summary

For any talent management plan to work, it should include three components – a focus, objectives, and actions. The focus of the plan identifies the problem it's designed to address and the employees it targets, based on an organization's talent needs.

Plan objectives are clear goals based on the focus you identify. They should be clear and measurable, as well as realistic.

Actions are the steps identified for achieving objectives. They should be carefully scheduled and have specific outcomes that can be measured against the objectives.

# TALENT MANAGEMENT: ACQUIRING TALENT

Most organizations know the importance of having effective recruitment and hiring processes. They know that – to be successful and remain competitive – they need to recruit and select talented individuals.

However, many organizations don't put enough time and effort into these processes. As a result, these organizations operate without well-considered or effective talent acquisition strategies.

Competitors who **have** given due importance to recruitment will expose this lack of foresight when they get hold of the best talent, thereby gaining a competitive edge.

Acquiring talent is one of the key components of a talent management strategy.

In this course, you'll learn these strategies that enable you to effectively recruit and select talented individuals for your organization:

- determining the appropriate talent acquisition approaches in different situations
- implementing a talent-focused recruitment strategy, and
- selecting talented individuals who'll fit into and contribute significantly to your organization

By applying these strategies, you'll be better equipped to acquire the talent your organization needs to support its objectives.

This can have results for both your organization and you personally:

- it can give your organization a critical advantage over the competition, and
- it can contribute to your success as a manager

## Acquiring the Right Talent

1. Approaches to Talent Acquisition
2. Implementing a Talent-focused Recruitment Strategy
3. Selecting Talent

# APPROACHES TO TALENT ACQUISITION

1. Internal versus external acquisition

Companies can acquire talent in two main ways. They can build talent internally by developing it in their existing employees. And they can obtain talent externally, by recruiting new employees.

Which approach is best?

The answer depends on your company's situation. Both approaches have specific pros and cons, and these make them suitable in different cases.

When you acquire talent internally, you need to determine what talent your company needs and identify existing employees who have the skills. It then involves taking steps – like providing coaching or mentoring – to convert these employees' potential into the talent that's required.

Choosing to develop talent in existing employees has several advantages:

- it demonstrates commitment to your employees and their career development
- it makes use of existing knowledge that employees have developed over time with the company, and
- it improves leadership retention

**Demonstrates commitment**

If you show commitment by investing in the development of existing employees, they're likely to respond by showing their dedication and commitment to your organization. The positive work atmosphere that this creates can result in higher productivity and lower staff turnover.

**Uses existing knowledge**

Existing employees have built up knowledge about your company, its values and standards, and the way it operates. Also, some skills and behaviors can be learned only on the job.

The tacit knowledge that existing employees already have may take months or even years for new employees to acquire.

**Improves leadership retention**

When you develop existing employees, you prove that your organization recognizes, appreciates, and rewards long-term commitment. And the longer employees stay with you, the more they'll develop and become leaders within the organization.

Conversely, hiring new employees may send the message that you don't believe in the potential of your existing employees. This could discourage employees from staying long or striving for leadership roles.

But acquiring talent by developing it in existing employees also has disadvantages. It requires that you set up an effective development program, and this can be time-consuming and expensive. Also, once it's set up, the program has to be maintained and remain a high priority for your company if it's to be successful.

Another disadvantage of relying on an internal development strategy is the risk of becoming too internally focused. If this occurs, a company tends to measure the strength of its talent only by its own historical standards.

For example, the company might ask itself whether its managers are getting stronger over time, rather than asking questions related to the market – like "How would our managers compare if forced to compete for their own jobs against the best external candidates?"

If a company fails periodically to compare its performers to those of outside players, it risks falling behind the competition over time.

Finally, having an effective development program that produces highly talented employees means you're at risk of losing this talent to competitors. If an organization has a strong track record in turning out talented leaders, it's likely executive recruiters will consider it a good hunting ground for talent.

Question

Tim's advertising company needs to appoint three new project managers within the next six months. It chooses to develop existing employees who've shown management potential, instead of hiring project managers externally. It helps that the company's recently invested in a development program for top talent.

What are the advantages of this approach?

**Options:**

1. The selected employees are likely to be highly dedicated
2. The employees are already familiar with the advertising company's standards and ways of operating
3. It encourages potential leaders to be committed to the company
4. The company lessens the risk that competitors will try to poach its employees
5. The company will maintain its competitive edge over time by focusing on internal talent

Answer

**Option 1:** *This is a correct option. Demonstrating commitment to existing employees by investing in their skills and career development encourages dedication in return.*

**Option 2:** *This option is correct. Existing employees have tacit knowledge they've gained through experience in working for the ad-*

vertising firm. New employees who are hired externally still need to acquire this knowledge over time.

**Option 3:** *This is a correct option. Developing existing employees is a sign that their company recognizes, appreciates, and rewards long-term commitment.*

**Option 4:** *This option is incorrect. Tim's company may lose employees who excel in leadership because they become more attractive to competitors, which increases the risk of poaching.*

**Option 5:** *This is an incorrect option. Internal development doesn't guarantee competitive advantage, because it's not always the best approach to take.*

Acquiring talent externally involves identifying your company's talent needs and then employing new people who can meet these needs. It involves a full recruitment process – attracting and interviewing suitably qualified candidates, and selecting the best candidates to hire.

**Acquiring talent externally**

When a company needs to replace someone quickly, hiring externally is often the best approach.

Many people find that when they hire employees from outside the company, they strengthen the leadership team and bring in valued competencies.

Recruiting externally means you can acquire new talent quickly. This is particularly helpful when you need to find individuals for senior-level leadership positions or when your internal development efforts have just started.

Sometimes it's just easier to recruit someone from the outside who has the needed talent and experience, rather than to try to develop internal potential.

Searching for talent outside your organization can strengthen your existing leadership team because you bring in talented individuals with other valued competencies. For example, if an organization wants to be more innovative, it may import managers who share certain key competencies or values in this area. And by acquiring talent externally, the company sends a strong message about the types of leadership behaviors it thinks are of key importance.

Recruiting new talent makes it more likely your company will stay competitive. This is because it enables you to assess and choose from the talent that's currently available in the marketplace.

In addition, the introduction of strong external job candidates can force complacent employees to be more competitive.

Question

David's top risk analyst has just resigned from his investment company. He chooses to search externally for a new risk analyst. His organization doesn't have an established development program.

What advantages can this approach have?

**Options:**

1. The new analyst may introduce new ideas or ways of working and inspire existing employees
2. David will be able to replace the risk analyst more quickly than by developing potential talent in the company
3. David keeps himself up-to-date with the best talent in the risk analysis market
4. David is able to strengthen the existing leadership skills in his team
5. David will develop existing employees' careers indirectly
6. The new risk analyst is likely to be more reliable than an existing employee who's developed to fill the role

Answer

*Option 1: This is a correct option. Bringing a new risk analyst into his company can initiate a culture change because the new recruit may expose existing employees to different and innovative ways of thinking.*

**Option 2:** *This option is correct. Developing talent in existing employees takes time. When David recruits a suitable risk analyst, the new employee already has the required talent.*

**Option 3:** *This is a correct option. If David's company doesn't employ external candidates from time to time, it can easily lose track of the types and levels of talent available in its industry and so fall behind its competition.*

**Option 4:** *This option is correct. By employing external candidates with good leadership skills, David can strengthen the leadership potential of his company.*

**Option 5:** *This is an incorrect option. Choosing to acquire talent externally is an alternative to developing that talent in existing employees.*

**Option 6:** *This option is incorrect. Acquiring talent externally is more risky than developing talent among existing employees. This is because external candidates are unknown – there's no guarantee of their reliability.*

Disadvantages of acquiring talent externally are that recruiting and searching externally can be very costly for a company and sometimes disruptive. Employing new, unknown candidates is also risky.

Select each disadvantage of acquiring talent externally to find out more about it.

## Costly

The recruitment and selection processes can be expensive, and so hiring externally becomes costly. Existing employees slowly work their way up an internal salary escalator. However, attracting external talent away from a competitor may require companies to offer a higher salary than if they were to hire internally.

Other costs to consider include relocating new recruits or providing severance packages for employees displaced by new hires.

**Disruptive**

Acquiring external talent can be disruptive. For example, if you hire multiple new employees, it can mean ordinary operations will be disrupted until these employees have learned what's required and have settled in.

To help with this, you can create a changeover plan and ensure both existing and new employees are happy with the changes. If you don't, some existing employees might quit, especially if they feel their jobs are no longer secure.

**Risky**

Acquiring new employees is always risky because you can't know for sure they'll be able to perform the required jobs or are reliable. Also, new employees may fail to fit in with your company's culture and standard ways of operating. If this happens, they may choose to leave.

You can't eliminate these risks, but you can make your recruitment process as effective as possible in finding people who best fit the positions you need to fill.

2. How to select the right approach

Both approaches to acquiring new talent have pros and cons. The best approach depends on a variety of factors specific to your company's situation and talent needs. And often it's best to use a mixture of the two approaches – in which case, the decision you need to make is what balance of the two approaches is best.

Factors outside your organization can also help determine which approach is best.

For example, if the economy is in a slump, it may mean that few jobs are available but there's surplus talent. It will then be easier to acquire the best talent externally.

When demand for talent in the market is high and available talent is in short supply, companies may tend to develop talent internally because it's cheaper.

## Question

However, a company can't always choose which approach to use.

In which cases do you think this occurs?

**Options:**

1. When potential for developing the required talent internally doesn't exist
2. When the required talent is highly specialized and specific to the company
3. When marketplace competition for the required talent is fierce
4. When only the company and its direct competitors require specialized skills

## Answer

*Option 1: This is a correct option. A company may need to acquire talent that it can't develop internally, for example because it's changed its strategic focus or direction. A company branching into specialized research and development in a new field, for instance, may lack the internal potential for developing the required talent.*

*Option 2: This option is correct. If a company is extremely specialized in what it does, it's possible it won't be able to find the talent it requires externally. It may then have to develop the potential talent among existing employees.*

*Option 3: This is an incorrect option. Even if marketplace competition for talent is high, a company may succeed in attracting this talent externally – or it may choose to focus on developing the talent internally.*

*Option 4: This option is incorrect. If there's only a small pool of companies that require specialized skills, it's likely the talent pool will be small. While this increases the competition for talent, it will still be possible to either hire externally or develop talent internally.*

For a company that does have a choice, four factors influence which approach is best:

- the length of time for which the talent is needed
- whether there's an existing ladder of skills and jobs within the company
- the company's current culture, and
- the likely accuracy of future predictions about the company's demand for specific talent

If you know you're going to need particular talent over the long term, it can be best to search for and develop that talent internally.

When you invest in the development of existing employees, you encourage their loyalty and dedication, and help ensure you get a return on your investment.

Candidates who are promoted from within may be more committed and loyal than external hires. In addition, the promise of promotion is a great retention device.

The more skills and jobs exist within your organization – especially within functional areas – the easier it becomes to develop talent internally. A ladder or hierarchy of skills and jobs enables candidates to learn through internal development. However, if required skills and jobs aren't available at various levels of your organization, you may need to acquire talent externally.

Before choosing how to acquire talent, you should consider your company's current culture. Do you think it needs a change? Or perhaps it's working well and you really don't want it to change.

If you're happy with the company's existing culture, it may be best to develop needed talent internally, using a steady development program.

If you want to initiate a culture change, however, you may want to acquire talent externally. New employees can reinforce the new values and behaviors you want to promote.

Finally, consider the accuracy of your predictions about the needs of the talent you want to acquire. The more uncertain your predictions are, the riskier it becomes to invest in developing the talent internally. If you're unsure how long your company needs the services of a particular talent, it's probably best to acquire it externally.

Certain factors indicate the direction that you should lean in acquiring talent – whether it's to develop internally or hire externally. Select each approach to learn why it's best for a particular situation.

**Develop internally**

A large and functionally oriented company may tend toward talent development. Such a company is likely to have long product development cycles and reasonably predictable needs for talent. It also has the scale – including many different levels of competencies – that's required to make development efforts effective.

**Acquire externally**

Companies that find it difficult to forecast how their needs will change may hire externally or outsource for some of their work – for example, IT work. They may not have the scale or depth in a given functional area to develop required competencies internally. And it may be risky and costly to do so.

**Job Aid**

Criteria for Choosing Your Approach

**Purpose:** *Use this job aid to help you determine whether to acquire talent internally or externally.*

Consider four main factors when determining whether you should acquire talent internally or externally.

**Length of time you need the talent**

If you know your organization is going to need specific talent over the long term, it's generally worth investing in developing that talent internally. This will result in more dedicated employees who are likely to stay with the organization. If the talent is needed only over the short term, it's better to acquire it externally.

**Existence of a hierarchy of skills and jobs in your organization**

If there's an existing ladder of skills and jobs that will enable employees to learn through development, it's appropriate to hire talent internally. If these skills don't already exist, it's better to look for talent externally.

**Culture status**

Bringing new people into an organization can affect its culture, because the new people bring new ideas and ways of doing things with them. So acquiring talent externally may be appropriate if you want to re-invigorate or change your company's culture. If you want to maintain your company's culture or if it's a particularly strong culture to which outsiders may have difficulty adjusting, it may be preferable to develop required talent internally.

**Future predictions**

If future predictions about a company's direction are uncertain – and it's therefore uncertain how long particular talent will be required – it's generally best to acquire that talent externally. If predictions are more certain, it may be worth investing in developing talent internally.

Question

By considering certain factors, you can determine which approach to use to acquire needed talent.

Match each situation to the best approach. Each approach will have more than one match.

**Options:**

A. Your department needs talented product developers to help the organization move into several new product markets

B. Your organization is uncertain of its future IT talent needs, and doesn't have the capability to develop the required IT competencies

C. Your organization has too much talent in its high-potential program and wants to keep up with the competition by bringing in new ideas

D. Your department needs to maintain its present culture

**Targets:**
1. Internally
2. Externally

Answer

*You should search internally for new talent if you want to develop your existing staff complement and you're sure you need the talent for a length of time. It's also better to search internally if you want to maintain the culture particular to your organization.*

*If you have too many talented internal candidates for available positions, it may limit your ability to hire externally to bring in talent with new ideas. In this case, you might cut the number of people in your high-potential program and hire externally. In addition, if you're uncertain about the demand for talent, it's a good idea to hire externally to reduce the risk and cost of internal development.*

3. Summary

A company may acquire talent externally or by developing it internally. Each approach has specific advantages and disadvantages.

To determine the most appropriate approach in a given situation, you should consider the length of time for which particular talent will be needed and how accurate your future predictions about this are. You should also consider whether there's an existing hierarchy of skills in your company and whether you want the company's current culture to change. Sometimes it may be best to use a mix of the two approaches.

# IMPLEMENTING A TALENT-FOCUSED RECRUITMENT STRATEGY

1. Brand recruiting

If your company chooses to acquire talent externally, its success largely depends on an effective recruitment strategy. It has to be able to find and attract the right kinds of talented candidates.

Traditional recruitment methods include offering internships, using job service agents, posting advertisements, and participating in job fairs.

In addition, a range of new, more innovative recruitment methods have become popular:

- web sourcing – or attracting talented candidates for positions via the Internet
- networking – or making connections with people in all fields to learn what's out there
- conducting information seminars – which allows candidates to learn about the operation of the company and its values
- using head-hunters – which helps pinpoint the best talent that is available in the market, and
- employee referrals – which encourage existing employees to recommend candidates who can meet spe-

cific talent needs

Question

Why do you think many companies have adopted new and innovative recruitment methods?

**Options:**

1. They want to beat the competition for the best talent
2. They recognize that traditional techniques are ineffective
3. There's been a dramatic change in the types of candidates companies want to attract

Answer

Companies have adopted new approaches to find, employ, and retain the best talent.

*Option 1: This is the correct option. Increased competition for talent has led many companies to adopt more innovative recruitment methods. With high demand for talented people in the modern marketplace – and not always the supply to meet it – you can't hope for talent to come to you. Instead, you need to go to them and ensure they identify your company as an attractive place to work.*

*Option 2: This is an incorrect option. Many traditional recruitment techniques are still used and can be effective. Often these are combined with newer, more innovative techniques.*

*Option 3: This option is incorrect. Companies want to attract candidates with talent. Although the types of competencies called for in the modern workplace may differ from those previously in demand, it's not this that has led companies to adopt new recruitment techniques. What has changed is the extent of the competition for people with valuable talents.*

Given high competition for talent, it's important to develop an employer brand or image.

The candidates you want to attract should be able to identify with the employer brand you develop. This enables them to decide whether they'll be a good fit in your company and lets them know what your company has to offer.

What is important is how the brand image draws on your organization's unique strengths and beliefs to appeal to the kind of talent pool you want to recruit and retain.

Using a brand to attract talent is a strategy that successful recruiters are leveraging. Characteristics that companies tend to emphasize in their brands are an appealing work environment, growth and learning opportunities, and the chance to make an impact.

**Appealing work environment**

Your employer brand should demonstrate why your company is an appealing place to work. You might describe the perks your company offers – for example, performance bonuses or a free lunch on Fridays for everyone. Or your company might focus on how its culture stresses sharing and openness, or how it emphasizes innovation and creativity.

One way to convey the appeal of your work environment is to give job candidates an introduction to the organization that emphasizes what life will be like if they join. A realistic preview helps set realistic expectations and can drive away individuals who won't be a good fit.

**Growth and learning opportunities**

An employer brand that stresses growth and learning opportunities can be effective.

To attract talent, an organization should emphasize how individuals who join it can build careers or learn more skills. For example, an organization might point out how much it has spent on educating its employees as part of its brand.

**Chance to make an impact**

Talented individuals select organizations that have a positive image in the marketplace and the community. For example, they may search for organizations with a good record of social responsibility or established environmentally friendly practices.

New employees want to represent a successful employer and want to be associated with it. A company that gets a good review from the general public is very appealing for new talent.

An example illustrates how to create a good brand image. A consulting company emphasizes it has been the leading consulting firm for over a decade. This tells potential candidates that working for the company will give them a chance to make an impact, because the company itself has an established position as an industry leader.

The company also highlights its practice of allowing employees to pursue relevant degrees while working and of giving them company stock on completion of degrees. This skill-building offer will appeal to talented individuals who are keen to develop their careers.

To portray the work environment, the company creates a video that features employees from all functions and levels explaining what they do and why they enjoy their work. It also provides job applicants with copies of company attitude survey results, indicating how employees feel about working for the company.

Question

Which are examples of how to convey an effective employer brand image?

**Options:**
1. Describe the environmental projects the company has successfully implemented
2. Stress that work at the organization is fast yet fun, and colleagues are friendly
3. Give examples of how executive team members started their careers at the bottom and rose through the ranks with experience
4. Advertise vacancies on networking web sites
5. Offer advice to people who've been fired to ensure they don't say negative things about the company

Answer

**Option 1:** This is a correct option. Many talented individuals like an organization that engages in beneficial social and environmental projects. Emphasizing your company's environmental responsibility is effective because it gives your company a positive public image.

**Option 2:** This option is correct. Talented individuals are attracted to working environments that appeal to their personalities and needs. Many talented individuals are attracted to a company that's highly productive, yet at the same time fun and friendly.

**Option 3:** This is a correct option. Talented individuals want to progress in an organization. By emphasizing your company's record of promoting from within and its growth and learning opportunities, you tell the prospective employee they can build a career at your company.

**Option 4:** This option is incorrect. Placing advertisements on networking sites is a way to recruit candidates for vacancies. It's how you describe the company that conveys the employer brand image.

**Option 5:** This is an incorrect option. Fired employees are unlikely to say positive things about the company no matter what you do, and this may only make them feel worse. This is not the time to try to improve your brand image.

2. Implementing a talent-focused strategy

To recruit appropriate talent for your organization, you need to develop a talent-focused recruitment strategy. You create an employee value proposition, stress career opportunities, attract passive as well as active candidates, and create a talent hub.

An employee value proposition – often referred to as an EVP – consists of what an employer promises its employees. For employees, it answers the question "If I come to work here, what's in it for me?"

The focus of an EVP is often confused with an employer brand. An EVP does contribute to the employer brand and draws from it, but it isn't the same thing.

To develop the right EVP, you need to understand the organization's current and future talent needs, in the context of its business strategy.

An EVP identifies the unique policies, processes, and programs that demonstrate an organization's commitment to employee growth and recognition.

It includes elements like compensation, benefits, affiliation, career, and work content.

To lure talented candidates to your company, your EVP should describe, amongst other things, how you distinguish yourself from the competition in terms of the rewards you offer, your management style, and the culture of your company.

**Rewards**

To develop an effective EVP, you might ask how the rewards your company offers distinguish it from the competition.

For example, you might state that your company offers a three-month sabbatical after ten years of service.

**Management style**

In your EVP, you should address the question of how to manage employees and processes better.

For example, you might explain that team members are encouraged to solve problems on the spot, encouraging autonomy.

**Culture**

You should describe what makes your culture special in your EVP.

For example, perhaps your company creates an inclusive culture by providing part-time employees with stock options. Or maybe it has a policy that requires employees to address each other on a first-name basis, which reinforces an informal culture.

Many organizations make the mistake of stressing job responsibilities and required skills when seeking new talent.

But it's important to remember that talented people typically seek positions that provide career opportunities. So to attract and retain them, you should highlight career opportunities.

Your job descriptions need to be descriptive and compelling, pointing to the challenges involved, some of the big projects employees will likely be part of, how these will impact the company, what employees will learn, and how employees will grow.

Say you're advertising the position of operations manager. Don't focus on what your company wants in terms of skills and qualifications. Rather, focus on what's in it for prospective employees. Catch their attention by appealing to their desire for better jobs and improved personal satisfaction. Then focus on career growth opportunities – outline the opportunities for promotion and how they can achieve them.

Another way to implement a talent-focused recruitment strategy is to make sure you attract passive as well as active candidates. Passive candidates are fully employed and may be very satisfied with their work, so it takes effort to attract them. You may need to sell your company and its diverse offerings and benefits. It's easy to get caught up in your own goals, but to reach these candidates successfully, it's important to focus on mutually rewarding relationships.

And remember it's common for passive job candidates to do quick, periodic job searches to check for new and interesting opportunities.

They may do so as a result of particular events, or because of something they hear or read that sparks a desire to do a search.

This provides a key opportunity for you to get these passive candidates to take notice of your business. You may need to be creative in your recruitment tactics.

For example, you might use communication forums to reach out and discuss your organization or your industry at large. Or you could publish occasional articles about your business. The more information you can provide, the better.

But it's also important to ask questions about what it is passive candidates are searching for. This will enable you to merge your opportunity with their employer wish lists.

Question

An organization is implementing a talent-focused recruitment strategy.

Match each example to the technique it illustrates.

**Options:**

    A.    It builds relationships with top people who aren't actively seeking jobs by setting up online forums about its business

    B.    It describes the training and responsibilities the successful candidate will have

    C.    It makes it clear that the new employee will be working with a friendly and efficient team

**Targets:**

    1. Attract passive candidates
    2. Stress career opportunities
    3. Create an employee value proposition

Answer

*Candidates who aren't actively seeking employment may still do searches from time to time. Establishing contact with them and then building a relationship can help this organization attract top people in the future.*

*Increasing responsibility and training are growth opportunities. Talented candidates aren't just searching for a job they know they can do. They're often searching for career opportunities, learning paths, and challenges.*

*To attract the talent to its company, the organization needs to make it clear that it's offering an all round experience – not just good money, but also an enjoyable and educational experience.*

Another way to implement a talent-focused recruitment strategy is to create a talent hub. A talent hub is a web site or web page that you use to present your employer brand and to specify career opportunities associated with working for your company.

Talent hubs aim to attract people to a class of jobs, such as marketing or finance.

Other sites may prompt job seekers to search for more specific job ads – such as those for a marketing manager – or to sign up to hear about future opportunities.

**Class of jobs**

Searching according to a job category in a talent hub will bring up all jobs available within that category. This means that candidates can explore all jobs that might appeal to them, based on their fields of interest. So even if they don't find the specific jobs they're searching for, they might be interested in other positions your company has to offer.

*The Diallonic talent hub displays, in which the Marketing category is selected and three results display – marketing team lead, marketing director, and assistant marketer.*

**Specific job**

If your company web site allows visitors to search only for specific job titles, it's likely you'll lose out on recruiting some talent. Candidates may search for jobs that reflect their skill sets, but not know the job titles you've used to describe positions. These candidates will miss the opportunities you're offering and search somewhere else.

*An example of Brocadero's job search engine finds zero results for specific job search – that of marketing manager. The user is requested to "Please try searching for another title."*

People who come to a talent hub should be able to register their level of interest and join a community of prospects.

If they choose to, they should be able to quickly upload their resumes.

And once the resume is "read" by the system, it will automatically generate a list of appropriate and available opportunities.

**Job Aid**

# TALENT MANAGEMENT

## Implement a Talent-focused Recruitment Strategy

**Purpose:** *Use this job aid for ideas on how to implement a talent-focused strategy.*

To attract and acquire the best talent for your company, you should implement a talent-focused strategy. There are four ways to do this.

### Create an employee value proposition

An employee value proposition is the total value for potential employees of working for your company, based not just on salary but also on factors such as working in an efficient team, learning from leaders, training in new fields, work satisfaction, and opportunities for increased responsibility. It's important that you offer an attractive employee value proposition so that your company remains competitive in attracting the best talent.

### Stress career opportunities

It's important to stress career opportunities when advertising positions. Many talented individuals value challenges and opportunities for building their careers, and are more likely to be attracted to your company if these are offered.

### Attract passive candidates along with active ones

Passive candidates are fully employed and may be very satisfied with their work, so it takes effort to attract them. You may need to sell your company and your diverse offerings and benefits to them. It's easy to get caught up in your own goals, but to successfully reach these candidates, it's important to focus on mutually rewarding relationships. You may need to be creative in your recruitment tactics. For example, you might use communication forums to reach out and discuss your organization or your industry at large. Or you could publish occasional articles about your business. The more information you can provide, the better.

### Create a talent hub

A talent hub is a web site or web page that enables prospects to search for available positions with your company and to find out about the opportunities your company offers. It's best to enable people who visit the hub to search for positions according to their fields of interest.

Catherine is a talented prospect who specializes in account management. Your talent hub is one of the first web pages listed in the results when she conducts an Internet search for jobs in her field. She browses it for positions that might suit her skills, but there's nothing currently available.

So Catherine chooses to receive updates whenever new positions within her field of interest do become available in your company. She later receives an update telling her that a position is available for an account project manager – so she applies for this position.

This means you have caught a talented prospect before she starts to show interest in other companies.

Question

You're currently implementing a talent-focused recruitment strategy for your company.

Match each example of a step you take to the corresponding technique.

**Options:**

A. Point out that your company offers $1,500-per-year college scholarships to each child of any employee who has more than two years of service

B. Create job descriptions that highlight how a person will be challenged, as well as what learning and growth opportunities are available

C. Provide information about your company to candidates who aren't actively seeking employment but who do the occasional search

D. Develop a web site that describes the career opportunities at your company

TALENT MANAGEMENT

**Targets:**
1. Create an employee value proposition
2. Stress career opportunities
3. Attract passive candidates
4. Create a talent hub

Answer

*Talented people want to know how they'll benefit from working for your company. This goes beyond offering competitive salaries. Non-traditional rewards, like college scholarships, are good incentives to attract and retain talented people.*

*Talented individuals will be attracted to positions that provide them with opportunities for challenges and building their careers.*

*You should focus on attracting not only active candidates, but passive ones as well. Building relationships with individuals who aren't actively seeking employment can increase your talent pool.*

*A talent hub is a web site or page that enables a potentially wide audience to search for positions and read about the benefits of working for your company.*

3. Summary

Developing an employer brand helps ensure the success of your company in recruiting talent. This brand communicates the benefits associated with working for your company and gives potential candidates a good idea of whether they'll be a good fit in the company.

To implement a talent-focused recruitment strategy, you need to create a competitive employee value proposition, stress the career opportunities that your company is offering, attract passive as well as active candidates, and create a talent hub.

Follow-on Activity

Is Your Company Talent-focused?

**Purpose:** *Use this follow-on activity to determine how talent-focused your company is.*

**Instructions for use:** To use this tool, consider your company's most recent talent search and then answer the questions.

- What do you offer in your employee value proposition?
- What career opportunities do you offer?
- What strategies do you have for attracting passive candidates?
- What strategies do you have for attracting active candidates?
- Has your company created a talent hub? If not, how could you get started in doing this?

# SELECTING TALENT

1. Identifying interview benefits

The entire recruitment and interviewing process requires a great deal of careful thought. That's because it culminates in a selection decision. It's critical to focus on how this decision is made, who makes it and when, and whether it will be accepted.

Consistency is important in interviewing and selecting talented candidates.

What would happen if you were to subject candidates to unequal treatment, or if interviewers were to have ulterior motives?

Others may challenge the validity of the final choice. Some candidates may feel victimized, and the decision will be impossible to justify.

The interview is accepted as an employment rite of passage – one that every candidate must go through in order to get a job. It's important that candidates experience it as fair and impartial. This creates goodwill among all candidates and helps ensure your organization attracts future talent based on its reputation for being fair.

In addition to being fair, an interview experience should leave a lasting, positive impression of the organization, whether the candidate receives and accepts an offer or not.

Some organizations approach their candidates in the same way as they approach their customers. In other words, they make sure that candidates receive the same quality experience that the organization expects to deliver to its customers – for example, warm, welcoming, considerate, knowledgeable, and involved.

Question

Which do you think are benefits of being able to conduct effective interviews that result in the selection of talented individuals?

**Options:**

1. You'll ensure new employees are a good fit with your organization
2. You'll avoid the time, hassle, and expense that comes with hiring a candidate who's a poor fit
3. You can recognize unsuitable candidates immediately and disqualify them by asking them more difficult interview questions
4. You'll complete the recruitment process and appoint new employees faster
5. You'll add to the reputation of your organization as one that attracts and secures the best talent

Answer

*Option 1: This option is correct. Effective interviewing makes it more likely that you'll select the best candidates for positions – those who are most suitable for the available positions and who will be a good fit with your company.*

*Option 2: This is a correct option. Rectifying a poor fit can be costly, time consuming, and require departmental restructuring. Conducting effective interviews helps you identify the candidate who will be the best fit.*

*Option 3: This option is incorrect. All candidates should be treated equally and fairly during the interview process.*

*Option 4: This is an incorrect option. Interviewing effectively saves time and money in the long run by helping ensure new employees are a good fit with your company. However, it doesn't enable faster recruitment – effective interviews take time to plan and conduct.*

*Option 5: This is a correct option. Finding talented individuals through effective interviewing will ensure that you hire the talent you need. In turn, you'll contribute to your organization's reputation for attracting the best talent.*

Effective interviewing has several benefits:

- it enables you to find a candidate who is a good fit with your organization
- you can avoid the need for inconvenient and disruptive changes that come from trying to incorporate a new employee who's a poor fit, and
- you'll enhance the reputation of your organization as one that attracts and gets the best talent

**Find a good fit**

A good fit means that the individual you select is the one best suited to your organization and to the job. Candidates who are a good fit are those whose ambitions, style of work, and personality enable them to perform excellently – and to become productive quickly – in the new job. With employees who are good fits, you'll experience lower staff turnover.

**Avoid disruptive changes**

Effective interviewing can prevent disruptive changes to your department or organization that come with placing an ill-fitting hire. Compensating for a bad fit can mean departmental restructuring, time wasted on training and development programs, and even the expense of having to start the recruitment process again from scratch.

**Enhance reputation of organization**

When you effectively interview and pinpoint the relevant talent for your area of responsibility, you help not only your department perform well, but also the entire organization. It also has the effect of building your reputation and that of the organization as one that attracts and secures the best talent out there.

2. Effective interviewing

In past years, recruitment agencies, newspaper ads, job fairs, and graduate recruitment programs were the major tools for attracting talented individuals to organizations. Now less traditional methods are used – for example, recruitment web sites, information seminars, talent scouting, social and business networking, and monitoring current affairs for talent.

But despite changes in recruitment processes, organizations today still regard interviews as the key selection method.

As such, the recruitment team should plan interviews carefully and develop clear objectives.

Specific techniques can help you interview well and find the talent that's a good fit with your organization. First you must ensure you define the job for which you interview candidates. Then, during the interview, you should provide a realistic job preview and discuss the criteria that will make for a good fit.

3. Defining the job

The first step in effective recruitment is knowing exactly what you want from candidates – in other words, the characteristics that enable them to do the job well. To figure this out, you need to accurately define the job for which you're hiring.

One way to define a job is to write an accurate job description. This typically includes a brief description of the job, a list of responsibilities, and required skills and qualifications.

When job descriptions read like shopping lists of requirements, they often reveal their inherent disadvantages. They exclude potentially suitable candidates, fail to fully clarify what a job entails, and fail to attract candidates.

**Exclude suitable candidates**

A job description may prevent potentially suitable candidates from applying if it sets out unnecessary skill or experience requirements. Also, the presence of a skill or qualification on a candidate's resume doesn't automatically mean that person can do the job.

**Fail to clarify what a job entails**

A list of skills and even a short description can fail to clarify exactly what a job entails. Skill requirements are usually quite general. But even specific requirements like the knowledge of a particular software package or a particular area of industry give no impression of the day-to-day activities involved in a job.

**Fail to attract candidates**

A job description may fail to attract potential candidates if it doesn't present an enticing impression of the job. The potential for career development, for doing appealing work, and for making an impact are strong motivators for talented candidates to apply for a job. A mere list of required skills fails to promote a job.

A good way to define a job is to create a prioritized list of what a person in the job needs to do to be considered successful. This list describes the main performance objectives, plus the critical sub-tasks the person must perform.

It defines the job – not the person you think should fill the position.

And a job advertisement that describes the challenges rather than the required skills is more likely to attract top performers.

It's easier to reach consensus when job descriptions focus on what people need to do, rather than on what people need to have.

You won't be as constrained by having to meet artificial and sometimes unnecessary requirements.

Moreover, your assessment of candidate competency will be more accurate.

A completed list of performance objectives lists the key results required in order of priority, mentions the critical processes or steps used to reach these results, and provides an understanding of the company environment.

You can assess candidates' competencies and motivation by obtaining detailed examples of how they achieved similar objectives in the past. These examples help you find top performers by matching their motivating interests and skills directly to real job need.

Question

Which are effective ways to define a job?

**Options:**

1. By listing the qualifications of an ideal candidate
2. By listing the ideal candidate's skills and personal qualities
3. By listing the most important tasks the successful candidate must perform to reach the job's performance objective
4. By listing the job results the successful candidate will be expected to achieve
5. By clarifying job expectations during the interviewing process

Answer

**Option 1:** *This option is incorrect. You can define a job more effectively by describing objectives related to job performance rather than by listing required qualifications. Qualifications don't clarify what the job involves and may prevent potentially suitable candidates from applying.*

**Option 2:** *This is an incorrect option. A job can't be defined clearly through a list of required skills or personal attributes because this gives little indication of what's actually involved in performing the job.*

**Option 3:** *This option is correct. A list of tasks that the successful candidate will have to perform as part of a job gives potential candidates a clear idea of what the job will involve.*

**Option 4:** *This is a correct option. An effective job definition should define the objectives that need to be achieved to be successful at the job.*

**Option 5:** *This is an incorrect option. You need to clarify what the job requires before you start interviewing so that you know what you're searching for in candidates.*

## 4. Providing a realistic job preview

Many new recruits leave their positions because they started work with unrealistic ideas of what their jobs would entail. To help ensure a good fit and to give prospective employees a clearer idea of what working for your organization is like, you should provide them with a realistic job preview.

An effective job preview helps dispel any misconceptions by specifying what candidates can expect and what will be expected of them.

You can provide a job preview during an interview. You should explain what the job requires and point to the career advancement opportunities associated with the job.

Some companies may also offer internships or job shadowing. These can be an ideal way for candidates to learn what working for these companies will really be like before they're appointed to longer-term positions.

You can conduct a realistic job preview with a group of several candidates or in one-on-one interviews.

Throughout the process, candidates learn about what the organization can offer and can assess how the opportunity matches up with their expectations.

A preview should cover topics that are typical areas of misunderstanding between new hires and organizations – for example, how quickly the candidate can progress up the corporate ladder, the level of responsibility the candidate will have, the opportunity to grow personally through training, how secure the job is, and the degree to which the candidate can be creative.

You should also discuss job-specific criteria such as the nature of the position that's on offer, the job's key objectives, the value to the organization of tasks the candidate would be expected to perform, and the levels of autonomy, repetition, and variety involved in doing the required work.

**Job clarity**

Job clarity refers to the degree of certainty or risk required to be successful in the new position.

**Autonomy**

You should let candidates know what level of autonomy – or independence – to expect in the position you're offering.

**Task value**

Task value refers to the priorities of the performance tasks an employee needs to carry out in order to meet job standards.

This helps determine the level of responsibility associated with the position and the relative priorities that the employee must give to different tasks.

**Repetition**

It's important for candidates to know whether a job consists of repetitive work, with specific tasks or processes that must be regularly repeated.

If this is the case and you don't let candidates know, the person you appoint may become frustrated soon after being employed.

**Variety**

Just as you should let candidates know whether repetitive work will be required, you should tell them how much variety of work to expect in the offered position. Candidates can then decide whether they'll find the position sufficiently stimulating.

A job preview can continue into the start of a new recruit's employment period.

Open, frequent follow-up discussions help to clarify and update obligations and expectations.

Question

Which are effective ways to provide candidates with a realistic job preview?

**Options:**

    1. Distribute a printed leaflet describing the benefits of

## TALENT MANAGEMENT

working for the company

2. Ask each candidate to spend a few hours with an employee working in a similar position to the one that's being offered
3. Focus on the negative aspects of working in the position on offer to weed out candidates who are weak performers
4. Discuss the level of responsibility that the candidate will have and the amount of coaching and mentoring the successful candidate will receive

Answer

**Option 1:** *This option is incorrect. A realistic job preview should enable candidates to determine how well they'd fit into an organization. A list of benefits would be more suitable in an employment offer or in an employer brand.*

**Option 2:** *This option is correct. Job shadowing is one way to give potential employees a clear idea of what it will be like to work in your company.*

**Option 3:** *This is an incorrect option. The purpose of a job preview is to give candidates a realistic idea of what it's like to work for your company and of what the job entails. It doesn't mean focusing on the negative aspects. This could put candidates off pursuing the job.*

**Option 4:** *This is a correct option. Covering topics such as these will help the individual figure out whether the job is a good fit.*

5. Criteria for a good fit

There are three components of job fit you should consider when assessing each candidate:

- person to organization – the criteria needed for a good fit between a candidate's objectives and those of the organization
- person to culture – or what will make for a good fit of a candidate to the organization's culture, and
- person to person – or what's required for the candidate

to fit in well with existing employees

**Person to organization**

There's a good person to organization fit if a candidate's work history and goals align to the work required to deliver the products and services of the organization.

To determine a person to organization fit, you should explore personal work characteristics, such as flexibility, innovation, being a quick learner, resourcefulness, and dependability.

Take the example of an architect joining an architectural firm with organizational goals focused on creating innovative structures. One of the reasons the new architect is a good fit is because her personal goal is to be creative and daring in her architectural designs.

**Person to culture**

A good person to culture fit exists if a candidate's work style fits in with the prevailing norms – or culture – at the organization. An organization can define its culture by taking note of employees' general behavior and ways of working.

For example, it's a norm in a financial consulting company for employees to work overtime and cope with intense work pressure and tight deadlines. Candidates for a position should be aware of this so they can choose whether working for the company will suit them.

**Person to person**

There's a good person to person fit if a candidate is likely to work and interact well with existing employees.

Employees are more likely to consider leaving if they don't get along with their colleagues or clients. It's also important to note that a new employee who creates workplace tension can reduce the productivity of others.

Say an advertising agency includes many chatty, outgoing, and dynamic employees who maintain a fairly informal office environment and strengthen their team spirit by socializing after work. Any new recruits who are less socially inclined might struggle to fit in well with their colleagues.

Once a preferred candidate has been selected, you need to make this person an attractive offer to ensure your company secures the required talent.

While most people consider salary to be the biggest motivating factor in accepting a job offer, other factors – like the opportunity for advancement, an excellent organizational reputation, a good work environment, and dynamic coworkers – also count, particularly for talented individuals.

Question

Which are considerations for establishing whether a candidate will fit with your organization and with the job on offer?

**Options:**

1. How well a new recruit will get along with the staff at a new place of work
2. How long a candidate will take to commute to a new place of work
3. How do a candidate's values and ambitions align to the values and objectives of the organization
4. How the candidate's lifestyle and style of work will fit with the organization's culture
5. How much a candidate currently makes

Answer

**Option 1:** *This is a correct option. A person to person criterion is very important in establishing a good fit.*

**Option 2:** *This is an incorrect option. While this may be a factor in overall job satisfaction, it wouldn't affect how well a candidate fits into a new job.*

**Option 3:** *This option is correct. The person to organization fit is a large part of determining a good fit.*

**Option 4**: *This is a correct option. The person to culture fit describes how a person will fit in with the style and working life at an organization.*

**Option 5**: *This option is incorrect. This would be a matter to discuss as part of an offer of employment.*

6. Summary

Benefits of effective interviewing are that you'll be better able to ensure a good fit between the selected candidate and your organization, and you'll avoid the need for potentially expensive, time-consuming adjustments once a selection decision has been made.

For a selection process to be effective, you need to define the available job clearly, provide candidates with a realistic job preview, and discuss the job-specific and organization-specific criteria that will make candidates a good fit for a position.

# TALENT MANAGEMENT: DEVELOPING AND ENGAGING TALENT

Whether your organization measures success by profit margins or customer satisfaction, that success is directly tied to employee satisfaction. If your employees are unhappy, they won't be as productive – so to be more successful, you need more satisfied employees. And to achieve this, you need to pay more individual attention to your employees.

Creating satisfied employees isn't just about increasing their benefits. It also means taking an interest in their personal career goals and development. You need to find out whether they find their current work challenging and engaging, and whether they're aware of development opportunities within the organization.

Question

Think about the employees in your sphere of influence. What level of commitment do they have to their work and to the organization?

Options:

1. Very high
2. Moderate
3. Low

Answer

***Option 1:*** *It's great if your employees are highly committed. But there's always room for improvement. Elements of this course can help you think about how you currently develop and engage individuals.*

***Option 2:*** *Your employees are only moderately committed. This course can help you improve levels of employee commitment in your sphere of influence by effectively developing and engaging individuals in your organization.*

***Option 3:*** *If your employees aren't very committed to your organization, this course can help you turn that around so you can effectively develop and engage individuals in your organization.*

This course will help you to develop and engage talented employees. It guides you through setting up an onboarding process – or orientation program – for new hires. And it shows how your onboarding process can be a framework for employees to use in building successful careers.

The course also details the steps you take to create individual employee development plans, and how to hold employee development discussions to produce the best results.

You'll also receive tips on how to engage employees so they perform at their best.

## Developing and Engaging Talent

1. Onboarding New Talent
2. Developing Talent in Your Organization
3. Engaging Talented Individuals in Your Organization

# ONBOARDING NEW TALENT

1. Why the onboarding process?

New hires face several challenges. Among these challenges are managers who are unavailable or who provide inadequate instructions and support. New hires may also have to deal with disorganized workflows, or a lack of training on the specific tools needed for their job.

Managers have a crucial role to play in bringing new hires on board, and it's important they make a good first impression.

Remember that new hires rely on you, as manager, to guide and direct them in the first weeks of their employment. This is known as onboarding – or introducing new employees to their new roles and responsibilities, setting goals and expectations, and acclimating them into the organization's culture.

Question

Research shows that how people start out in an organization strongly affects how they continue. How will you benefit from onboarding new talent effectively?

**Options:**

1. You'll have employees who contribute more quickly
2. You'll have clearer communication with new hires
3. You'll keep employees for longer
4. You'll find people who fit in well with your organization
5. You won't have to be involved as much with new hires

Answer

**Option 1:** *This option is correct. Onboarding helps talented employees get oriented faster, so they begin performing sooner. It helps minimize the downtime you experience when new employees start out.*

**Option 2:** *This is a correct option. By sharing information such as performance expectations right away, you can reduce misunderstandings that could lead to the premature departure of a new hire.*

**Option 3:** *This option is correct. Bringing talent on board effectively can increase morale and reduce turnover by showing employees they're valued. So you'll retain a group of loyal and committed employees.*

**Option 4:** *This is an incorrect option. Careful recruiting will ensure you find people who fit in well.*

**Option 5:** *This option is incorrect. It's important to be involved with new hires and guide them through the first couple of weeks at work. For onboarding to be effective, you need to provide lots of input.*

A well-designed onboarding process not only ensures people have a positive orientation experience, but will hasten new employees' time to productivity, and improve retention. In addition, you'll establish effective communication with new hires from the beginning, encouraging and inspiring them as they start out.

2. Setting learning objectives

So how do you ensure that the onboarding process is a success? First, you need to understand its purpose. Your primary goals should be to convince new hires that they made the right choice, introduce them to the organizational culture, and provide a foundation for their career development.

**Convince new hires**

New employees should feel confident they've made the right choice by joining your organization.

Research shows that new hires who aren't won over during onboarding often start planning to leave during this period. Even if they choose to stay, they may disengage, put in less time and effort, and be less productive overall.

New hires want to know if their needs will be met and what, in turn, is expected of them. So you need to affirm that people are valued, help them feel safe, build a sense of connection, and ensure they feel welcomed.

**Introduce organizational culture**

Employees need to be introduced to the organization's culture – its way of doing things and its values. This builds a lasting connection based on understanding.

For people to bond with a new organization, they need to find values and ideals they can identify with. For instance, a person who values integrity wants to know that the organization does too.

For its part, the organization needs to ensure that new hires comply with regulations. You need to explain the company's strategies, hierarchies, and relationships so newcomers grasp where they fit in, what behavior is appropriate, and how to perform well.

**Foundation for career development**

The organization has to cultivate people's careers to develop its talent. When you plan around careers from the outset, you make the most of newcomers' talents, affinities, and resources.

In turn, new hires need to feel valued and supported in pursuing their hopes and dreams. The more help and encouragement you give them, the more they're likely to invest in your organization.

Onboarding usually involves practical, formal aspects such as filling out legal compliance paperwork.

When you focus on these legal compliance activities with new recruits, but don't do anything else to orient them, it's known as passive onboarding.

Unfortunately, a passive onboard is a lost opportunity to communicate with newcomers. Once the onboarding process is over, it's much harder to establish a meaningful connection with them.

To create an effective, proactive onboarding process that convinces new hires they made the right choice, introduces the organization's culture, and provides a framework for career development, you can take three important steps. First you set practical learning objectives. Then you can design an appropriate learning program. Another step is to assign someone to support the new hire in the first few weeks.

Learning objectives help you focus on what the new hire needs to be successful and happy in the first weeks of employment.

You want to avoid assigning "busy work" that has nothing to do with the person's job just because you're having a busy week, or because you haven't prepared properly.

Setting learning objectives will help you provide focused guidance.

Useful learning objectives during onboarding include clarifying the company's expectations; making introductions; outlining the history, vision, and structure of the organization, and describing benefits and growth opportunities.

**Clarifying company expectations**

You let newcomers know what's expected of them so they learn what they need to accomplish in future. This process should outline the job responsibilities of the new hire.

For example, a small news media company expects employees to put in overtime when needed to meet deadlines.

**Making introductions**

To ensure new hires feel accepted and included, you need to welcome new recruits and introduce them to their colleagues. This step is often forgotten, but it's an important part of learning about other employees, their work, and where they fit into the organization.

For example, a new sound engineer at an advertising agency is introduced to team members, industry experts, and clients.

**Outlining history, vision, and structure**

It's important to familiarize newcomers with how the company operates and what its values are. With this knowledge, new hires are better equipped to find where they fit into the organization's culture.

For example, a data clerk is shown how accountability works in the company's cross-functional teams and how this structure relates to the company vision of innovative products and employee empowerment.

**Describing benefits and opportunities**

New hires need to know what's in it for them if they are to remain with the organization. So it's important to explain in the onboarding process what the organization can offer them in terms of benefits and opportunities for career growth.

For example, a new lawyer for a large corporation is informed of stock options given for years of service and is told about potential growth paths within the company.

Question

A sales manager is preparing to onboard a group of salespeople for a large publishing house. When designing an onboarding and orientation program, what learning objectives should she set?

**Options:**
1. Explain the organization's general performance expectations and how she expects each new hire to help her meet organizational goals
2. Welcome new hires, and introduce them to their colleagues and their teams
3. Describe the team structure and the reporting structures within the organization

4. Let new hires know they'll get bonuses if they meet their sales targets
5. Ensure new hires have organized offices and workstations that are pleasant and comfortable to use
6. Reward good performances and initiative in new hires

Answer

**Option 1:** *This option is correct. Letting the new hires know what's expected of them is an effective learning objective to set because newcomers learn what they need to accomplish in future.*

**Option 2:** *This is a correct option. Welcoming new recruits and introducing them to their colleagues ensures they feel accepted and included.*

**Option 3:** *This option is correct. If they understand the structure of the organization, new employees will know how to work within it and maximize the benefits of its particular structure.*

**Option 4:** *This is a correct option. Informing people about benefits and opportunities helps them learn how the organization can further their careers.*

**Option 5:** *This option is incorrect. Although providing pleasant, comfortable workstations for people is important, it's not really a learning objective.*

**Option 6:** *This option is incorrect. Although rewarding good performances and initiative is vital for developing talent, it's not part of an onboarding and orientation program.*

3. Designing a learning program

Once you've set clear learning objectives, you can begin the second step of the onboarding process – designing a learning program. Learning programs are plans for practical activities designed to acclimatize newcomers to your organization.

Learning programs need to be holistic – they should deal with both social and performance-based aspects of bringing a newcomer on board.

Organizations tend to focus on performance needs when designing a learning program. They provide training manuals and explain how to do things.

However, organizations often overlook the social aspects of orienting new employees. Yet these are essential for building lasting, meaningful relationships.

So what types of practical activities should you include in learning programs for new hires? To provide a holistic program, you need to give plenty of advice, offer a mix of training activities, and provide a centralized information store.

**Advice**

Advice has both performance-based and social aspects. Useful tips and practical know-how are invaluable when training people for new positions. For example, a new editor needs to be familiar with the style guides used by an organization.

Advice is also a wonderful opportunity to build connections with people – to discuss what they need to know, what they're worried about, and how they can master specific problems. For example, a new editor may need tips for dealing with a difficult author.

**Mix of training activities**

A good mix of activities helps improve retention and focus. There are many training techniques you could use. For example, training manuals are useful for standardizing processes and enabling good performance. You can also create individualized e-learning programs.

However, learning also needs to have a human face. So you should also include workshops, individual mentoring, and one-on-one encounters in the program.

**Centralized information store**

A centralized support site that clarifies company processes can provide employees with a simple method of finding all the information they need.

Intranets can also provide an opportunity to connect online with other employees, which helps develop a sense of community.

Question

How comprehensive is your company's learning program to on-board new talent?

Options:

1. Very comprehensive
2. Moderately comprehensive
3. Very limited

Answer

**Option 1:** *If you're offering a thorough, varied program that deals with both social and performance-based aspects, you're likely to raise the quality of new talents' work and build meaningful relationships with them.*

**Option 2:** *A good learning program should be thorough and varied to cover both the social and performance-based aspects of onboarding. Think about how you can boost the quality of your learning program.*

**Option 3:** *Unfortunately, a program that isn't thorough and varied is unlikely to be effective. So new talent may not produce high quality work or establish meaningful connections with your organization.*

4. Employee support

A good learning program is enhanced by assigning someone to provide support to a new employee during the first few months. A designated "buddy" can help new employees learn essential information and meet people, so they get off to a quick and successful start. This frees you, as manager, from the time-consuming tasks of anticipating and answering new employees' basic questions.

You should ensure that people playing this supportive role are also supported.

They should have space in their schedules so it's clear that their support role is important.

You can reward buddies with bonuses or other forms of appropriate compensation for their effort.

When you assign a buddy to a new hire, consider your organization's needs, the new hire's capabilities, the type of position being filled, and the business environment. Who should you deploy? When? What will the new hire need help with?

**Who should you deploy?**

Buddies should be slightly more experienced, but more or less equally ranked as the person they're going to support. This means the role isn't the same as that of a mentor. A mentor is someone who has advanced far along an employee's chosen path and who can therefore offer guidance and advice to the employee with regards to that path.

You should supervise buddies early during the working relationship, and monitor how the relationship is progressing. If it's not a fit, you should assign a new buddy.

**When?**

No matter what the context, buddies need to be available right from the start. So assign them well before newcomers begin work. Buddies should check in with new hires several times during the first year.

Buddies need to play a strong supporting role during the first week and be available in a lesser capacity for the rest of the year. This support should be both social and performance-related.

**What will hire need?**

Buddies need to provide a warm and friendly welcome. They should provide introductions to the team and familiarize new hires with the building and equipment.

Buddies should also provide tips on how to complete tasks and be available to answer questions as they arise.

When you bring people on board successfully, you ensure that the first impression they get of your organization is a positive one.

You establish a relationship, and you lay the foundation for developing and engaging their talent for many years to come.

**Job Aid**

Steps for Successful Onboarding

**Purpose:** *Use this job aid to guide you in planning and implementing the onboarding process.*

To establish an effective, proactive onboarding process that accomplishes the objectives of convincing new hires they made the right choice, introducing organizational culture, and providing a framework for career development, you can take three important steps:

**Step 1 – Set learning objectives**

First you should set clear learning objectives for the program. Learning objectives help you focus on what the new hire needs to be successful and happy in the first weeks of employment.

Useful learning objectives during onboarding include clarifying the company's expectations; making introductions; outlining the history, vision, and structure of the organization; and clarifying the benefits and growth opportunities.

**Step 2 – Plan a learning program**

Once learning objectives have been set, you need to provide a practical, holistic learning program for new employees, so they quickly become socially acclimated to your organizational community and are equipped to meet performance requirements. Learning programs should include the following key components:

- **advice** – helps employees master their new responsibilities effectively and perform better. It's also crucial for helping them feel included, supported, and valued as new members of the organization.
- **a mix of training activities** – should be aimed at teach-

ing people how to work, stimulating their interest, standardizing performances, and providing a human face for the learning process.

- **a centralized information store** – should be available to new hires. This serves as an ongoing reference guide and ideally can also be used for social networking within the organization.

**Step 3 – Assign support**

Finally, you should assign a buddy to support the new hire during the first months of work. When assigning a buddy, bear in mind the buddy:

- should be a peer – more experienced but equally ranked
- should be assigned before the new hire starts work and continue to be available for advice and discussions for several months
- needs to provide both social and performance-based support and will also need to be evaluated and supported
- needs to be warm and friendly, provide general information, guide the newcomer around the work environment, and give tips and advice on how to do the work assigned

Question

Suppose you manage the IT Department for a news agency.

What would you need to do to set up an effective onboarding process for a new web content coordinator?

**Options:**

1. Set overall goals for understanding content needs, learning the company web policy, and training in the current management schedules for the site
2. Plan coaching sessions, e-learning modules, and work-

shops that'll help the new employee work effectively and become involved with other team members
3. Ask the other web content coordinator to help the new person understand the organizational culture of the news agency
4. Assign a mentor to show new hires around the agency and to provide tips on how to manage the web site
5. Set up a group feedback session to provide corrective feedback to the new hire after one week of work

Answer

**Option 1:** *This option is correct. You need to set clear learning objectives when setting up an onboarding process.*

**Option 2:** *This is a correct option. You need to design a comprehensive learning program to bring someone on board effectively.*

**Option 3:** *This option is correct. You should assign someone to support the new employee when bringing that person on board.*

**Option 4:** *This option is incorrect. You should assign a peer as a buddy to show the new hire around the agency and provide tips. This frees you up to focus on your managerial responsibilities.*

**Option 5:** *This is an incorrect option. Although regular one-on-one feedback may be useful, a group feedback session would be very stressful for a new hire.*

5. Summary

Onboarding helps new hires understand new responsibilities, roles, colleagues, and the organizational culture. When onboarding is successful, job satisfaction and employee retention increase. This boosts the performance of your department.

To ensure a successful onboarding process, you first need to set learning objectives in line with departmental goals. Design a learning program that is varied and that encompasses social and performance aspects of the job. You should also assign people to support new hires during their first year of employment.

# DEVELOPING TALENT IN YOUR ORGANIZATION

## 1. Developing employees

Many companies spend a lot of time and effort on attracting and selecting talented people. But then they just sit back and wait for the rewards that the new talent will bring. This approach isn't effective. You need to think about how to inspire and motivate new employees and how to provide an environment for them to develop their talents further. You want to improve their long-term performance through development and training.

Employee development is a long-term commitment to provide individuals with work experience that prepares them for greater responsibility in the future. Typically, about 90% of employee development is done on the job.

Training, on the other hand, is a short-term intervention designed to give employees fast access to the work knowledge and skills they need to perform their tasks. Its focus is on making employees productive as soon as possible.

Managers aren't always expected to play a large role in training, but should be deeply involved in employee development.

Training is expensive and isn't enough to prepare people for promotion. So development is both important and a cost saver. Because most development occurs on the job, it's under a manager's direct control. As a manager, you can use a range of development methods such as coaching, talent-review discussions, feedback, and stretch assignments.

Question

Under what conditions do you think learning is most effective?

**Options:**
1. When it's integrated into employees' projects, roles, and everyday work experience
2. When it's strategic, intentional, and self-led
3. When it occurs off-site
4. When it occurs in large groups

Answer

Learning is most effective when it's integrated into an employee's everyday work experience and is strategic, intentional, and self-led. People learn when they take risks, and they learn from their interactions with one another.

Together with their direct reports, managers or immediate supervisors need to determine gaps that may exist in an individual's competencies.

A Strengths, Weaknesses, Opportunities, and Threats – or SWOT – analysis is useful here.

Then they should plan work experience to fill these gaps and build the competencies employees will need to perform well as their responsibilities increase.

2. Development plan goals

To help you determine development needs, you should co-create a career development plan with each individual you manage. This plan should outline the short-term goals for the employee's current position and the long-term goals for future work. It should also list the actions and experiences needed for the employee to meet these goals.

Creating an effective development plan requires that you hold a development discussion with relevant employees.

This discussion is a negotiation about what actions are needed to achieve business and personal goals.

A development discussion typically follows a number of steps. You need to describe business needs, identify current skills and areas of expertise, identify the employee's career goals, determine and prioritize competency and skills gaps, and outline practical action steps to fill those gaps.

Victor manages a programming team for a software development company. Follow along as Victor describes business needs to Lili, a junior programmer who shows excellent promise, at the start of a development discussion.

> **Victor:** To create an appropriate development plan for you, it's important to link the organization's goals with your own personal goals. One of the challenges we're taking on this year is breaking into the automotive industry.
> *Victor says seriously.*
>
> **Lili:** Yes, that's going to be very exciting. But the quality of our coding has to be impeccable.
> *Lili smiles.*
>
> **Victor:** Uh huh. Especially with the move towards smart cars. Our programs have to be reliable, because they have very real safety implications. Do you feel this change in focus could potentially help you grow and meet your own career goals, Lili?
> *Victor responds animatedly.*
>
> **Lili:** Definitely! I'm very interested in embedded software. There are lots of interesting possibilities around debugging this type of software, and it's a good career move for me.
> *Lili seems enthusiastic.*

Question

Considering what Victor said, what do you think a manager should cover when describing the needs of a business?

**Options:**

1. Explain the company's direction
2. Discuss the next year's business challenges
3. Link employee development with business needs
4. Find out about the employee's qualifications
5. Discuss customer trends and industry regulations

Answer

You should outline the company's future direction, discuss business challenges in the coming year, and directly link the employee's development with business needs.

When describing business needs in the development discussion, it's important to clarify the company's future direction so employees can think about how they may need to develop in order to move with the organization.

You should also list any challenges the organization will face in the coming year – in other words, what are the short-term goals of the organization?

Employees' success will depend on finding a balance between the meeting the needs of the organization and of individuals.

Once you've clarified business goals, it's useful to identify employees' current skills and expertise. This can help them set realistic goals for the future and helps you identify capabilities they may be able to build on. And for development plans to be effective, it's important to ask questions and to consider experience, as well as skills and competencies.

**Ask questions**

You should ask what tasks, roles, and responsibilities your employees are enthusiastic about, what they're struggling with, and what skills and capabilities they're currently using.

You may also ask employees to assess their own strengths and weaknesses.

**Consider experience**

Qualifications and skill sets recorded on paper aren't the only indicators of potential development directions.

Many successful people weren't originally trained in their fields. So always try to build development plans around the experiences and passions of each employee.

For example, a software engineer could tell you that she spends 20% of her time dealing with team motivation and personal dynamics. It may be more useful for her to develop her motivational and interpersonal skills, rather than her technical knowledge.

After you encourage employees to think about their skill sets and experience, you can help them identify their career goals. You should ask about their interests, getting them to focus on areas in which they would like to move. You should also explore their short-term goals and long-term career aspirations.

**Interests**

It's important to help employees develop their careers in a direction that will be interesting to them. You also want their interests to align with their strengths and with the strategic goals you defined earlier in the discussion.

It can also help to introduce employees to key contacts in their areas of interest. They might speak with these contacts, or create a mentoring relationship with them.

**Aspirations**

You can encourage employees to discuss their short-term and long-term career aspirations. You also explore the types of responsibilities that they expect to take on during their career. For example, you could find out whether employees want to advance in their current career path, move into a new one, or assume a management position.

You help employees come up with specific priorities, and agree on possible timeframes for achieving them.

The discussions should also cover an exploration of how employees can attain excellence in their current jobs.

# TALENT MANAGEMENT

Victor is having a development discussion with Lili, who has shown great talent at troubleshooting software. Follow along as they have a development discussion around her interests and aspirations.

> **Victor:** You say your technical knowledge and your attention to detail are your greatest strengths. What do you enjoy most about applying those skills in your current capacity?
> *Victor looks warm and encouraging.*
>
> **Lili:** Well, I enjoy analyzing and finding elegant fixes for the bugs. It's really engrossing and challenging – and that works for me.
> *Lili looks happy and motivated.*
>
> **Victor:** Sounds like problem-solving and debugging are what really interest you. Do you have any ambitions in that direction?
> *Victor asks with curiosity.*
>
> **Lili:** Well, I'd like to keep up with the new methodologies that are being applied to solve the problems that are coming up as technology develops.
>
> **Victor:** I think that's something our development program can help with. What kind of timeframe do you have in mind for gaining these skills?
> *Victor smiles.*

Victor asks helpful questions to find out more about Lili's strengths and goals. He discusses building on her experience in problem-solving and coding. He encourages her to think about her career interests. Then he moves on to discuss how her aspirations to consult could be realized, and what timeframe she has in mind. By paying attention to each of these aspects, he helps her create an appropriate development plan.

Question

Suppose you manage the financial analysis team for an investment company. You're having a development discussion with

Alice, one of your analysts.

Match each example of what you might cover during the discussion to the corresponding step. More than one example may match a single step.

**Options:**

A. Explain the company has to widen the range of industries it invests in to reduce overall risk

B. Find out what Alice would like to achieve in the next few months

C. Explore which types of analysis and research Alice finds most rewarding

D. Find out if there's a new career direction that she feels drawn towards

E. Find out what competencies Alice has that aren't being used

**Targets:**

1. Describe business needs
2. Identify employee's career goals
3. Identify current skills and expertise

Answer

*You describe business needs to link the employee's goals with those of your organization or department. You could discuss upcoming changes, or challenges the organization will face.*

*To identify employees' career goals, you ask questions about their short-term and long-term goals – as well as how their interests link with these ambitions.*

*To identify current skills and expertise, you might ask employees what they find rewarding and what skills and knowledge they currently have.*

3. Skills gaps and action steps

You've learned about the first three steps you take to create a development plan with an employee. For the rest of the development discussion, you should prioritize skills gaps your employee needs to fill before moving in the direction they have indicated, and then you can outline practical action steps to fill those gaps.

It's important not to rush this part of the discussion. Insightful questions can help people identify potential learning opportunities.

Remember how Victor and Lili discussed development plan goals, and looked at her career aspirations? To develop Lili's talent, Victor needs to prioritize the skills gaps she needs to address in order to move forward.

When he explores skills gaps with Lili, Victor establishes that her priority should be to deepen her understanding of the latest software-testing methodologies. She also needs to learn how to deal with problems specific to automotive software design, so she can grow with her organization.

Once you've identified the gaps that need to be filled for an employee to develop, you should outline practical action steps to realize them. You need to identify a few key issues to address, specify what actions to take and the outcomes the employee expects, and assign ownership for the action plans.

**Identify key issues**

For an action plan to be successful, you and the employee need to identify two or three key areas to focus on.

By keeping the number of key issues small, you ensure that the employee has sufficient focus and resources to really learn and change in those areas.

**Specify actions and outcomes**

Once you've identified key issues to address, you need to decide what to do about them - in other words, what actions to take and what outcomes you want. You discuss the best available ways to close the gaps, that best contribute to the employee's career aspirations and provide optimal results to meet current business goals.

You might, for example, discuss potential stretch assignments and job rotations that could help build competencies, skills, and knowledge.

Mentoring, coaching, and personal feedback are important ways to help employees reach the outcomes they desire.

**Assign ownership**

You assign ownership for action plans by determining which actions require your support or approval, and which actions the employee will carry out alone.

After the discussion, employees begin executing the plan, which typically outlines the activities they'll accomplish within the next 12 to 18 months.

You also need to periodically review and refine each plan to ensure that it truly addresses the ongoing developmental needs of employees.

Victor and Lili have identified and prioritized her skills gaps. Follow along as they develop an action plan.

> **Victor:** OK, so we know you need to know more about debugging embedded software in automobiles. What key issues do you think you need to focus on?
> *Victor is warm and open.*
>
> **Lili:** Actually, I suspect I'm going to need formal training in the field. I'll need a strong knowledge base if I'm to be effective in the long run.
> *Lili is thoughtful.*
>
> **Victor:** You're right Lili. We're going to have to invest in adequate training, because moving into the automotive software industry is a significant, long-term shift in our business objectives. Would you be interested in attending a series of workshops and in-house training courses around these issues?
>
> **Lili:** Definitely.
> *Lili thinks seriously.*

TALENT MANAGEMENT

**Victor:** We're setting up an ongoing training program over the next nine months. We're also bringing in a new senior programmer to oversee this specialized type of software development. How would you feel about working under a mentor?

*Victor responds seriously.*

**Lili:** That would be great. Training would give me a good foundation for working in the field, and having a mentor would be very helpful.

*Lili smiles.*

Victor's questions help Lili identify the key issues that need addressing. He suggests practical actions to address the gaps, but doesn't really discuss the desired outcomes. It's clear that the organization would like to take ownership of the process.

Question

You're having a discussion with a team leader, Maria, who would like to become advertising studio manager within a few years. She's very familiar with the specifics of the industry, but would like to oversee projects more effectively.

Match each example from the development discussion to the appropriate step. More than one example may match a particular step.

**Options:**

A.     Ask Maria what competencies she needs to develop to improve her ability to oversee studio productions

B.     Find out what skills would strengthen Maria's ability to lead her team

C.     Agree that Maria should focus on improving her project management skills

D.     Offer Maria coaching in compiling road maps for advertising projects

E.     Ask Maria to look into doing an online course in project management in her own time

**Targets:**

1. Prioritize skill gaps
2. Outline practical action plans
3. Assign ownership

Answer

*When determining and prioritizing skills gaps, you should ask employees to identify competency or skill gaps that they think need immediate attention in their current career development plans.*

*When outlining practical action plans, you need to identify a few key areas to focus on and prioritize the actions the employee needs to take to close skill gaps and move toward career goals.*

*You need to assign ownership by determining which action steps should be led by the organization and which ones the employee will take responsibility for.*

4. Summary

To develop talent effectively, you need individualized development plans. To create these, you have a development discussion with employees. During this discussion, you need to describe business challenges and goals and identify employees' career goals. This helps to ensure that personal and organizational goals are aligned.

You also need to identify employees' current skills and expertise, and to determine any skill gaps. You then determine action plans that address these gaps and that contribute to the employee's career aspirations and provide optimal results to meet current business goals.

**Job Aid**

The Development Discussion Guide

**Purpose:** *Use this job aid to guide you in individual development discussions.*

Use the following sets of lists to guide you through the development discussion.

**Describe business needs**
- outline business challenges in the coming year
- describe the future direction of the business
- link business needs to the employee's individual needs

**Identify current skills**
- What are the employee's strengths and weaknesses?
- What are the employee's current skills and tasks?
- What is the employee enthusiastic about?
- What does the employee do best?

**Identify employee's career goals**
- What are the employee's aspirations, priorities, and career interests?
- What expectations does the employee have?
- What are the employee's goals and timeframes?
- What relationships would be useful to the employee?

**Skill gaps and practical actions**
- What are the current gaps that need to be filled to meet career goals?
- Which gaps are priorities?
- What are three key issues the employee should address?
- What actions need to be taken?
- What on-the-job learning opportunities exist?
- What feedback, coaching, and mentoring opportunities are needed?

# ENGAGING TALENTED INDIVIDUALS IN YOUR ORGANIZATION

## 1. Engaging employees

No matter how good its engine is, a vehicle can't move forward if its gears aren't engaged. Even if your organization has the best talent available, it can't truly access this talent unless the individuals are engaged with the work and the organization.

To be engaged means you're interested. When a person is engaged at work, their own interests are aligned with those of the organization.

People who are engaged are dynamic, energetic, committed, and persistent.

They get fully absorbed in what they're doing, and think deeply about it. They're steadfast, because they believe in what they're doing, and they often pursue excellence for its own sake.

Isn't this the type of person you want at your organization? To get your employees engaged, you can use five strategies. You manage their work content, provide ongoing support, value and reward those people, create an enjoyable work environment, and meet employee expectations.

Question

Does your job description as a manager include the five tasks required for engaging employees?

Options:

TALENT MANAGEMENT

1. Yes, it includes all of them
2. It includes some of them
3. It doesn't include any of them

Answer

***Option 1:*** *Your job description includes all five tasks for engaging employees. That's great – your organization is definitely focused on talent development. This topic should help you hone your skills.*

***Option 2:*** *Your organization is genuinely trying to develop talent if some of these tasks are listed in your job description. This topic should help you expand on current efforts and further your own skills in getting the most out of talented employees.*

***Option 3:*** *If your job description doesn't include these tasks at all, your organization may not have a talent management process in place. This topic will guide you in terms of what's needed to engage talented employees.*

2. Managing and providing support

To engage talent, your first task is to manage work content so that it's challenging, enjoyable, meaningful, and provides some real level of satisfaction for employees.

There are several useful questions to ask when you want to determine whether work content engages your employees:

- Are these tasks challenging?
- Can the person get a sense of achievement from the work?
- Does it stimulate learning and growth?
- Does the person find everyday tasks meaningful? and
- Does work bring any kind of fulfillment for this particular individual?

There are three ways that you can manage work content effectively. First, allow for flexibility in how people work. Second, give employees more say in how to make improvements in their work, and third, match the content of work to individual capabilities and preferences.

Select each aspect of managing work content for more information about it.

**Allow flexibility**

Allow employees flexibility whenever possible by letting them choose how and where they work. Let them use job sharing if appropriate, and find creative solutions and compromises to suit individual preferences.

For example, someone whose work is entirely computer based may prefer to work from home, and may even be able to concentrate better and be more productive in a home-office environment.

**Give more say**

It's important to give people a say in how they work, and how they can improve their performances. This engages people – giving them ownership of their work – and utilizes their workplace experience.

For example, a salesperson is often best placed to suggest ways of increasing customer satisfaction and retention.

**Match content to individual**

When the content of people's work is matched to their individual aptitudes, competencies, and interests, they're more likely to find meaning, fulfillment, and purpose in their work. When you match employees to their roles, you optimize employee engagement and contribution.

For example, some employees might be well-suited to working with customers because they're better able to connect with others.

Victor is a manager at a large software development company. Martina has been with the company for a while. Follow along as Victor manages Martina's work content.

**Victor:** So, what you find most fulfilling about your work is

background coding in C++ and researching new technologies?
*Victor seems warm and friendly.*

**Martina:** Yes, that's right. I love the control of C++, and by learning about new technologies, I can find more elegant solutions.
*Martina seems enthusiastic.*

**Victor:** Are there any technologies you could recommend to the team?
*Victor seems interested and enquiring.*

**Martina:** There are two or three that might really be useful. I can send you the specs for them if you like.
*Martina seems confident and assertive.*

**Victor:** That's a good idea. Include where you think they'll best fit and I'll see what we can do. Also, let me know if there's any specific training you'd like – either around C++ or some of the new technologies.
*Victor is smiling and seems enthusiastic.*

**Martina:** I'd love to do that!
*Maria is smiling and seems happy.*

Question

How did Victor help Martina to engage with her work by paying attention to its content?

**Options:**

1. He found out what was fulfilling for her about her work
2. He asked for her opinion on how to incorporate new technologies into the team's work
3. He aligned some of Martina's tasks with her passions and competencies
4. He considered ways in which she could choose where and how to work
5. He identified her career goals

Answer

**Option 1:** *This option is correct. Victor identified C++ programing and researching new technologies as the source of Martina's fulfillment, so he found out what engaged her. Asking questions can help you identify what employees find engaging about their work.*

**Option 2:** *This is a correct option. By giving her a say, Victor helped Martina engage with her work by taking more ownership of it.*

**Option 3:** *This option is correct. By asking her to outline training that she might want and make technology recommendations, Victor matched the content of her work to her interests, so she became more intellectually and emotionally engaged.*

**Option 4:** *This option is incorrect. In this particular conversation, Victor didn't focus on helping Martina engage by giving her more flexibility in choosing where and how she worked.*

**Option 5:** *This is an incorrect option. Identifying career goals is a topic Victor might cover in another discussion, particularly when creating a development plan.*

Not only do people need physical resources to engage at work, they also need intellectual and emotional ones. Whenever resources are drained, the amount of energy that people can bring to their work will be limited – they'll be less engaged. But when you provide ample resources and support for coping with job demands and work–life stressors, you can restore the energy that enables people to engage.

When people experience too much stress, for too long, they burn out. Burnout often manifests in poor health, depression, inability to concentrate, or fatigue.

Often the most engaged individuals are the ones most prone to burnout.

Burned out employees who choose to stay are far less effective. Their energy and motivation dwindle, and their productivity and work quality decrease.

Providing support is essential to reduce workplace stress and burnout, thereby enabling employees to engage in their work. To provide support, you need to make sure there are adequate resources for coping, that the right training is available, and that working processes and conditions don't hinder individuals in their work. You should also try to give employees more control over the way they work and over their environments.

**Resources for coping**

Long hours, lengthy commutes, and inadequate diet and exercise routines drain people's resources. Look for ways to minimize these stresses.

You might also encourage employees to discuss emotionally-charged issues, such as ethical concerns or maintaining a work-life balance, and to work together to find solutions.

Keep people intellectually engaged by ensuring they understand the hows and whys of their work, keeping priorities clear, and offering help with problem-solving at work.

**Training**

When people know they can meet expectations, they aren't overwhelmed. So adequate training is a basic form of support. It encourages growth and development, which is key in keeping employees engaged.

And it helps employees to do their work well and in accordance with organizational standards.

**Processes don't hinder work**

Procedures and processes should enhance productivity. To prevent frustration, reduce needless protocols – such as unnecessary paperwork – and take advantage of technologies that minimize tiresome and repetitive tasks.

A familiar routine reduces stress, but when it's too monotonous, people lose interest. Try to create a balance between predicable tasks and new challenges.

Also ensure that employees can have a say in how to improve

processes and procedures that they work with daily.

**More control**

Top performers and critical talent will feel stifled if they are not empowered to make decisions about their work.

Giving people autonomy helps them feel respected, trusted, and responsible for their own projects. This promotes initiative and personal development.

One way to give employees more control over their working conditions is to let them select for themselves the technologies that best help them perform their tasks.

3. Valuing and rewarding

Valuing and rewarding people is key in encouraging engagement. Typically, people need more than just financial recognition. They're also driven by other types of rewards - ones that increase their sense of self-worth and job satisfaction.

An important emotional driver is fairness. Employees should clearly see that their performance is judged fairly and that their compensation reflects that performance.

Emotional recognition also goes a long way. You could create opportunities that allow employees to receive external recognition at conferences or industry get-togethers.

**Lili**

"At my last company, the manager commented only if you made a mistake, which was really disheartening. At my new company, Victor takes time to thank me when I do something well. He lets me know that when I do well, the whole company benefits. We create better products, we attract more customers, and I get a bigger bonus.

This really makes me feel like what I do is important and useful. The programs I help create make other people's lives and jobs better too."

**Curtis**

"My company is a large one and I'd always thought that would mean that there wouldn't be much interaction between me and my manager.

But my manager really pays attention. She gives me feedback on how I'm doing nearly everyday. So that's really encouraging. I know what I'm doing well and I get loads of advice on how I can improve and reach my goals.

It's personal here – not just business. That makes me feel noticed and appreciated. I know my career will develop here, because my manager is supporting me."

As Lili's enthusiasm shows, one of the biggest emotional drivers is each employee's perception that individual effort makes a difference. It's very simple for you to thank someone for their contribution and it doesn't take much time to do.

When you ignore talent or good work, employees sometimes disengage totally. They feel there's no point working hard because no one notices anyway.

Employees, particularly those at the start of their careers, expect managers to interact with them and provide feedback to help them meet their career goals.

As Curtis pointed out, frequent interaction and feedback helps employees feel noticed, appreciated, and on track. All this adds up to increased engagement with the organization and with its daily work.

Question

You work in an organization that provides skills training for people with disabilities.

Match each example of engaging employees to the strategy it illustrates. More than one activity may match a single area.

**Options:**

    A.    Allow employees to log status reports either manually or using automated processes

B. Provide bonuses for generating new and interesting workshop activities

C. Write thank you notes to employees who have managed difficult tasks well

D. Automate admissions processes to reduce tedious, routine tasks

**Targets:**
1. Providing support
2. Valuing and rewarding people

Answer

*Automating routine processes supports talented employees by reducing some of their workload, making their work more meaningful for them. You can allow employees to choose how they do their work to give them more control.*

*Linking performance clearly to compensation and showing your appreciation creates a culture of trust and respect for the individual, and is an important part of maintaining a high level of engagement among employees.*

4. Enhancing the work environment

Employees spend a lot of time at work. So the overall experience should be both interesting and appealing.

Successful companies engage talented people by creating a work experience that aligns with employees' needs and interests. They may offer an informal, free-spirited, and fun environment. Or they may create a sense of community by treating family, leisure, and personal well-being as important. Some companies even provide an on-site doctor or daycare facility.

You should spend some time finding out what your employees' needs and interests are and research their expectations of a good working environment.

Then you can make changes that enhance your employees' experience, making your department somewhere people want to work.

## IT company

An IT company realizes many employees need to develop their physical fitness because they spend extended periods sitting at computers. So the company sets up a gym room and a soccer club for employees.

## Retailer

A busy retailer realizes that the constant noise and busyness of the work environment is stressful for employees. So it creates a meditation room where employees can go to get some quiet.

The company also develops a process for employees to initiate and run a range of outreach programs, supported by the company. This helps develop team spirit and pride in the company and the work they do there.

Question

Suppose you are the manager of a large and busy clothing manufacturing factory. How could you enhance the factory environment for your workers?

**Options:**

1. Conduct a survey on what new facilities people would like to have provided in the factory
2. Set up a daycare center for the workers' pre-school children
3. Initiate a hockey team so employees can bond and improve their physical fitness
4. Provide training manuals to new hires
5. Put up a poster about workplace safety

Answer

**Option 1:** This option is correct. When enhancing a work environment, you need to find out what your employees' expectations, needs, and wants are.

**Option 2:** This option is correct. Setting up a daycare center would enable people to engage with work while knowing their children are *being cared for nearby.*

**Option 3:** *This is a correct option. Providing options for physical engagement and greater team spirit will improve the work environment.*

**Option 4:** *This option is incorrect. While providing training manuals to new hires will help them engage, it doesn't enhance the work environment.*

**Option 5:** *This is an incorrect option. Although a poster on workplace safety will help people follow correct procedures, it won't enhance the factory environment.*

5. Meeting employee expectations

How you meet employee expectations is crucial for engagement. If you want employees to feel positive about the organization, they must know that all people in the organization – even senior managers – share the same set of values. And what make these cultural values real are your intentions, promises, and actions.

So to meet expectations, you need to align your behavior with organizational values. And in doing so, you need to be authentic.

**Align with organizational values**

As a manager, you embody the core values of your organization. So your behavior should be in line with these values. This encourages employees to be more committed to the organization themselves.

The principles of your organization have to be expressed in what it actually does. If actions and principles don't match, employees lose trust and disengage.

For example, if you're part of a company that values diversity, but your department does not reflect this, your employees won't believe you hold this value.

**Be authentic**

If you aren't authentic, the people you lead won't trust you. So they won't give you real loyalty or feel morally and emotionally accountable to you. If you pretend to feel and think in a particular way – just because it's expected of you – people will quickly pick up on this.

Leaders need to personally align the organization's values, their own values, the promises they make, and the actions they take.

For instance, suppose you adhere to your organization's environmental principles, but you don't believe in what you say and do. Employees who really do care about the issue will inevitably feel betrayed when they notice your insincerity.

Victor's company provides IT support for Violet's organization. Over time, the two managers have become friends. Follow along as they discuss how they try to meet their employees' expectations.

> **Victor:** I find that as a manager, people expect a lot of you. I can't expect my developers to be creative, productive, and customer-oriented if I'm not.
>
> **Violet:** Oh absolutely. And I think it goes a lot deeper than that. I couldn't manage our organization if I didn't genuinely care about whether people are treated justly or not.
>
> **Victor:** Exactly. There's no point in trying to fake concern about the issues. Employees see through that in a second!
>
> **Violet:** One important value of our company is being aware of cultural diversity. I try hard, and I think clients from most cultures feel comfortable with us. Still, I do worry about making a mistake.

Both Victor and Violet know how important it is to really believe in the core values of their organizations, and to match their actions to their words. Organizational beliefs and values need to be built into the structures and processes of the organization in order to become operational. They also need to be communicated through messages about what people can expect of the organization. Finally, they are displayed in the day-to-day actions of people in positions of authority.

Remember that employees who are really engaged with the organization perform better and make the working environment more positive. By using the five strategies for engaging employees, you'll boost success in your department. And you'll find working there more enjoyable too.

**Job Aid**

Strategies for Engaging Employees

**Purpose:** *Use this job aid to provide you with ideas for engaging employees.*

You should think about five areas when you want to improve your engagement with employees.

**Work content management**

- allow for flexibility
- give employees more say in how to make improvements
- match work content to capabilities

**Support for dealing with the demands of the job**

- provide adequate training
- provide enabling technologies, and processes and routines that don't hinder work
- give employees more control over their working processes and conditions

**Value and reward people**

- be fair
- provide competitive pay and benefits
- help individuals feel their effort makes a difference
- communicate and give feedback regularly

**Create an enjoyable work environment**

- identify employees' needs, interests, and expectations so that the working environment is interesting, fun, and meaningful

**Meet employee expectations**
- make sure your actions and behaviors are in line with the espoused core values that the individual expects
- be authentic

Question

Your multinational retail chain has asked you to step in and manage one of its overseas branches. Many people are feeling mistrustful and alienated – largely due to your predecessor's mismanagement.

How could you improve engagement by meeting people's expectations?

**Options:**

1. Respect and accommodate the customs of local employees and customers in accordance with the espoused values of the overall organization
2. Make a point of rewarding excellence in accordance with the principles of the company
3. Take a course in the local language and customs to ensure that you're in line with the company's espoused values
4. Initiate a cycling team to represent the store and to build team spirit
5. Allow employees to work flexible hours

Answer

***Option 1:*** *This option is correct. You could improve engagement by meeting people's expectation that you'll be respectful and accommodating of cultural diversity, particularly if this is an espoused value of the organization.*

***Option 2:*** *This is a correct option. By matching your actions to the principles of the company, you meet expectations, and therefore improve engagement.*

***Option 3:*** *This option is correct. To be authentic, you need to align* your actions with your company's values.

**Option 4:** *This option is incorrect. Although the cycling team may enhance the work environment, it doesn't go toward meeting employee expectations in this case.*

**Option 5:** *This is an incorrect option. This is a way of engaging talent by managing work content.*

6. Summary

To be engaged with your work is to be interested in it. When people are engaged at work, their own interests are aligned with those of the organization.

Managerial strategies for improving employee engagement include managing the work content, providing support, valuing and rewarding employees, and enhancing the work environment. It's also important that managers meet employees' expectations, to build trust and respect.

**Follow-on Activity**

Ideas for Engaging Employees

**Purpose:** *Use this follow-on activity to guide you in brainstorming a list of ways to engage employees.*

**Instructions for use:** To use this tool, use this worksheet to brainstorm ways to engage your current employees. Print it out or create a worksheet of your own based on this layout.

| Template to discover some ideas | |
| --- | --- |
| What could you do to help your employees engage with your organization? | How will this motivate or engage them? |
| 1. I can manage work content by | |
| | |
| | |

| | | |
|---|---|---|
| 2. | I can provide support by | |
| 3. | I can value and reward employees by | |
| 4. | I can enhance the working environment by | |
| 5. | I can meet employees' expectations by | |

# TALENT MANAGEMENT: RETAINING TALENT

Consider the impact it has on your organization each time a talented employee leaves. This means losing valuable skills and expertise. You might replace the talent that's been lost by hiring someone new or by training existing employees to develop their skills. But in either case, the process is likely to be expensive and time-consuming.

Retaining talented employees is an ongoing challenge for most organizations. It's one thing to acquire talent and another to ensure your organization keeps that talent.

Employee resignations are nothing new, and neither are the types of reasons employees have for leaving a company.

For example, employees may choose to leave for any of these reasons:

- they're dissatisfied with their jobs or their bosses
- they're attracted by new opportunities available elsewhere
- they decide it's time for a career change
- they reach retirement age, or
- they opt to take breaks to study or travel

It's not always possible to prevent talented employees from leaving, but it is possible to take steps to make this less likely. To do this, you need to understand what makes individuals leave your organization and what strategies you can use to prevent this.

In this course, you'll learn the main issues and strategies relating to retaining talented employees in your organization:

- why talent retention is important
- how to determine what causes talent departures in your organization, and
- how to manage employees in a way that encourages talent retention

By applying the principles you learn, you'll be better equipped to retain talented individuals, which can result in happier, more committed employees, which in turn leads to better organizational performance.

**Retaining Talented Employees**

1. Importance of Retaining Talent in Your Organization
2. Determining Causes of Talent Departure
3. Strategies for Talent Retention

# IMPORTANCE OF RETAINING TALENT IN YOUR ORGANIZATION

1. The impact of staff turnover

In any organization, some staff turnover is natural. For example, people may retire, decide to change careers, or go back to college. But when top performers or critical employees depart their jobs – especially if this is happening often – you need to start worrying.

Like other employees, talented employees may occasionally leave your organization for personal reasons – over which you have little control.

Alternatively, they may leave due to dissatisfaction with factors specific to your organization – ranging from conflicts with managers to lack of recognition or too few opportunities for career development. In these cases, you risk losing more talented employees in the future.

And losing talented employees always has a negative impact.

For an organization, the negative impacts of losing talent include loss of expertise, loss of business, reduced productivity, and the direct monetary costs associated with replacing that talent.

**Loss of expertise**

When a talented individual leaves, your organization loses that person's expertise. This expertise may be difficult to replace –

for example, if the departing employee was particularly accomplished in a particular task, process, or system. If no suitably qualified replacement is found, the loss can harm the organization's product or service.

**Loss of business**

Sometimes customers may follow a departing employee, taking their business to the employee's new company. The loss of a talented employee could also leave a team short-staffed – preventing your organization from being able to accept specific business opportunities.

**Reduced productivity**

The loss of talented employees can reduce productivity, with fewer high-performing individuals left to contribute to the organization's overall output. Employee departures can also disrupt an organization's workflow, especially if the employees leave on short notice.

**Monetary costs**

Replacing a talented employee is costly. If you choose to recruit a new employee, your organization has to bear the costs of the recruitment process. Alternatively, it will have to carry the costs associated with developing the required talent in an existing employee. And in either case, the replacement employee will need time to adjust to the new position and may also need training – all of which have financial costs.

In addition to high financial costs, productivity losses, loss of expertise, and loss of business opportunities, staff turnover can affect the job satisfaction of remaining employees. That's because they may be forced to take on extra workloads or address problems associated with the departures.

They may also be distracted, trying to figure out why employees are leaving.

And yet another negative impact of high turnover is its effect on the image of the organization. It may be viewed as a company that can't hold on to its talent.

When talented employees leave, it not only affects the organization but also the individual who decides to go. Leaving a job can involve a loss of benefits and seniority, financial hardship, and frustration over wasted effort or uncompleted projects. It can also bring stress associated with making a transition into a new job.

**Loss of benefits and seniority**

A talented employee who leaves an organization loses benefits and seniority associated with staying with an organization over a number of years. Starting a new job almost always means starting over, because the employee may lose vested interest in benefits at their previous organization.

Moreover, for many employees, the workplace is their primary social network. Giving that up and moving to another organization often results in the loss of that network, along with its emotional support.

**Financial hardship**

Talented employees may not have lined up new jobs before leaving an organization – especially if they leave due to dissatisfaction or frustration. They may then face potentially extended periods of unemployment with no income.

**Frustration over wasted effort**

Talented employees who leave an organization are likely to be frustrated. They won't realize the results of the effort they've invested in projects that aren't yet completed. It's possible that without them the organization won't know either.

Employees who were particularly invested in their work can have difficulty handing it over to others. And when talented individuals leave, organizations may even cancel the projects they worked on or fail to continue recognizing their value.

**Stress**

Finding a new job and then fitting into a new organization is always stressful. Even a highly talented employee may struggle to find a suitable position and to adapt to the culture and ways of doing things in a new organization.

## 2. The benefits of staff retention

For managers and their organizations, focusing effort on retaining talent can have several benefits. These include operational improvements, better overall employee performance, and a more positive work environment.

Retaining talented employees can help you meet organizational goals by ensuring smoother workflows and reducing operational problems.

This is because the flow of work isn't interrupted by the departure of an employee and the arrival of a new employee, who needs time to reach required productivity levels.

Retaining talent also leads to improved quality of transactions with customers, which means better customer service and satisfaction. This happens because when you work to retain employees, you create more employee satisfaction, which in turn leads to positive employee behaviors towards customers.

By adopting strategies to encourage talent retention, you make it more attractive for employees to stay with your organization. For example, one of your retention strategies may be to provide excellent development opportunities for employees.

As a result of such strategies, you're likely to notice an improvement in staff commitment and job satisfaction.

In turn, this helps you get the most out of your employees, which makes it easier to achieve organizational goals.

And keeping talented employees contributes to a positive work environment conducive to professional development. This can lead to reduced office conflicts and less stress. You'll be able to avoid spending significant time and resources addressing the issues of disgruntled, departing employees.

Retaining employees also reduces the amount of recruitment you have to do – which saves you the financial costs of recruitment.

Less recruitment also reduces the delays and bottlenecks that new employees may cause while they're still learning.

An added benefit is competitive advantage. Retaining talented employees means you won't lose good performers to your rivals.

**Reasons for high staff turnover**

Organizations may cite a variety of possible reasons why talented employees leave. Common among these are that turnover is a general problem in the industry, the Human Resources Department isn't doing its job properly, or the organization's geographical location isn't attractive enough to keep talented employees from seeking jobs in more "exciting" cities or towns.

But talent departure isn't out of your control. It's not all externally driven – either by the industry or location. Most effective retention solutions are internally driven. And remember, turnover can still be low in organizations in geographical areas or industries where it's very difficult to attract employees.

A variety of myths about talent retention circulate, and these can prevent organizations from being proactive in trying to retain talented employees.

Some of these myths are that staff turnover isn't expensive; that turnover – even high turnover – is a normal cost of doing business; that turnover is positive; and that managers are powerless to do anything about turnover.

**Turnover isn't expensive**

Staff turnover can become very expensive, especially when the turnover is high. Aside from the direct costs of recruiting and training replacements, indirect costs – such as the time that senior staff or mentors must dedicate to helping each new employee settle in and learn the job – adds to lost production time.

**Turnover is normal**

When managers simply accept the idea that turnover is part of doing business and therefore unavoidable, they're unlikely to make proactive efforts to retain talented employees. Moreover, they won't analyze what went wrong when employees do leave, instead blaming the departures on a "normal" trend. Remember, the costs of business will be much lower if you can avoid talent departures.

**Turnover is positive**

When turnover isn't excessive, it can bring about positive changes – like rejuvenating the workforce and organization. However, when turnover of talented employees reaches high levels, the negative consequences – such as cost and productivity implications – far outweigh the positives.

**Managers are powerless**

Managers aren't powerless to prevent talented employees from leaving. Often, they're the most influential people in employees' working lives and can play a significant role in encouraging employees to stay.

Question

Two managers, Mimi and Sara, are talking about the high staff turnover at Sara's call center. Sara doesn't think it's a problem, dismissing it as a "standard" at her company.

What can Mimi say to convince Sara of the benefits of being able to retain talented employees?

**Options:**

1. "Did you know that employees perform better when employee retention is high?"
2. "Hanging on to your best agents can create a positive work environment."
3. "Retaining your most experienced agents will ensure success with your call center."
4. "If you could keep your best agents, you'd definitely be able to provide better customer service."
5. "Keeping your best employees is seen by executives to be a direct result of your management style."

Answer

***Option 1:*** *This option is correct. Retaining talented employees improves staff commitment and job satisfaction, which helps you get better performance from your employees. When you have good retention strategies, such as plenty of development opportunities, it follows that employees will get more satisfaction from their jobs.*

***Option 2:*** *This is a correct option. Retaining talented employees tends to reduce conflicts and stress in the work environment. Because employees are more satisfied, you have fewer disgruntled and disruptive employees. This makes your job, as well as everyone else's, more satisfying.*

***Option 3:*** *This is an incorrect option. Retaining your most experienced agents doesn't automatically mean your company will succeed.*

***Option 4:*** *This option is correct. Retaining talented employees results in better customer service and improved customer satisfaction because there's continuity of service.*

***Option 5:*** *This is an incorrect option. This self-serving attitude could actually create a negative work environment.*

3. Summary

Losing talented employees can cause an organization to lose expertise, business opportunities, productivity, and money. Because of this, managers should make dedicated efforts to retain these employees.

As well as avoiding the negative consequences, retaining talent can have several benefits for managers. These include operational improvements, better employee performance, and a more positive work environment.

# DETERMINING CAUSES OF TALENT DEPARTURE

1. Causes of talent departure

You might think you know why employees have left your company in the past, based on the reasons they gave you for leaving at the time. But do you really know the cause of why talented employees leave? Some of these reasons are probably highly specific to your organization or department. To prevent good talent from leaving, it's vital to discover what the reasons are.

Employees may provide one of many possible reasons for their departures. They might have personal commitments that have little to do with the job itself. Or they may leave because of external, industry-specific pressures, or because of internal problems with your department.

**Personal**

Sometimes the reasons employees leave are personal and have little to do with your organization. They might have family obligations that conflict with their jobs or transportation problems, or simply want to change careers.

**External**

Some reasons are external ones. New employees could receive counter-offers from their former employers, for example. Or other companies may offer your employees jobs with higher salaries or more career advancement opportunities.

**Internal**

A set of factors associated with your organization could make employees leave. They might dislike the work environment in your organization or find the work they're doing stressful.

They may have problems with their supervisors or working hours, feel unappreciated, or feel that they're not fairly rewarded for their contributions. They may also feel they're not allowed enough independence or flexibility in their day-to-day work.

Before you adopt strategies for retaining talent, it's important to investigate the real reasons why talent leaves your organization.

You don't want to waste time and resources by implementing inappropriate strategies. For example, it's common to assume that raising salaries will fix the problem. But if talented employees are leaving for reasons that don't relate to pay, this will be expensive but ineffective.

A good place to start is by assessing turnover records to determine any trends in who's leaving your organization.

You can examine the data with different categories or job characteristics in mind, such as gender, religion, age, level of experience, or job group. For example, you may find that turnover is highest in the Sales Department, among married females under age 30.

Once you've identified a trend, you need to determine what's causing it. This requires more exploration. It involves investigating why employees who fall into the high-risk category you've identified are more likely to leave than others.

Question

Once you've identified a high-risk group for talent departure in your company, how do you think it's best to go about exploring the causes for this?

Options:

1. Consult external HR specialists
2. Ask employees in the group you've identified

3. Brainstorm with other managers

Answer

**Option 1:** *Sometimes it can be helpful to ask expert consultants or refer to studies that point to the most likely reasons for staff turnover. But often the reasons for talent departure are highly specific to a particular organization or department. The best way to find out what these reasons are is to ask the affected employees directly.*

**Option 2:** *You're right to consult with your employees first – they're the ones who'll be able to tell you exactly why they're leaving or what might make them leave in the future. You can then pinpoint specific causes to deal with directly.*

**Option 3:** *It may be helpful to brainstorm with other managers, but there may be specific reasons for talent departures that you can discover only by going to employees themselves.*

It's important to go directly to your employees to find out what makes them stay in your organization, what external pressures might lure them away, and what internal problems might cause them to leave.

You can get this information from employees in several ways. You can use surveys and interviews to gather data and establish trends; focus groups and the nominal group technique to investigate causes; and exit interviews to discover exactly why employees choose to leave your organization.

2. Surveys

You use surveys to measure prevailing attitudes or opinions. For example, you can use them to test employees' job satisfaction, loyalty to the company, or perceptions of management. Surveys can also show how employees' attitudes change over time or how attitudes differ across departments or groups.

An advantage of surveys is that you can use them to gather information quickly, from a large number of employees. For example, you might ask all employees in a department – or in your company – to complete a survey on a particular day.

The content of a survey will vary depending on what information you're trying to gather.

For example, if you suspect talented employees are leaving due to general job dissatisfaction, your survey should ask employees about issues like individual recognition, whether they feel their work is appreciated, how they feel about their relationships with their supervisors, and so on.

You can categorize surveys into five main types, including routine and reaction surveys, surveys you use to analyze a particular problem, exit surveys, and impact surveys. Each of these has specific uses.

**Routine survey**

You use routine surveys on a regular basis – annually for example – to identify trends in employee opinions or attitudes. They're a good way to spot issues as they emerge.

**Reaction survey**

You use reaction surveys to measure employee reactions immediately after a major event or disruption occurs. You then evaluate the data and, if necessary, take action to prevent talent departure.

**Survey to analyze a problem**

You can use surveys to analyze problems after they're uncovered. For example, if you suspect there's general dissatisfaction with a new process, you could use a survey to help identify what it is about the process that's causing concern.

**Exit survey**

An exit survey is a short questionnaire you give to employees who are in the process of leaving the company – either just before or just after their departure. You use this type of survey to uncover employees' reasons for leaving.

**Impact survey**

You use an impact survey to evaluate the success of a talent retention solution after it's been implemented. If you made changes to a process because employees were dissatisfied with it, for example, you could use an impact survey a month or two later to test that employees are satisfied with the changes.

Using surveys can be effective, but to get the most out of them, you should ensure they have these characteristics:

- they should be simple and clear – you'll gather more reliable data if employees know exactly what's being asked of them
- they should be focused on getting the information you need and ask only relevant questions – if a survey is too long, employees might not take the time to respond fully
- they should be anonymous – employees may be more candid if their responses can't be traced back to them, and
- they should be designed to allow for comparison – for example, so that the prevailing attitudes in one department or group can be contrasted with those in other departments

Ensuring a survey is easy to complete helps ensure you get a good response rate. One way you can do this is by structuring a survey as a set of statements and asking employees to rate each statement based on whether – or how much – it applies to them. This makes it quick and easy for employees to provide their responses.

Scoring responses in this way also makes it easier to compare survey results – for example, from different departments or groups.

You can minimize resistance to a survey if you give employees advance notification that they'll be asked to complete it. Employees can then set aside time for doing this.

As well as keeping a survey as simple and relevant as possible, you should simplify the response process. For example, you could give employees the option of completing the surveys electronically or put a return box in a central location.

Question

Why do you think it's important that surveys are anonymous?

**Options:**

1. You're more likely to get truthful responses
2. You'll find it easier to assess responses
3. You'll get the surveys back more quickly

Answer

The main reason why it's important to ensure completed surveys are anonymous is that it makes it more likely you'll get truthful responses. Employees won't need to worry that managers will penalize them for any negative comments they make. It won't make the evaluation or completion of surveys easier or quicker.

It's also a good idea to include a signed introductory note to show that a survey is sanctioned by a top executive. This lets employees know that the survey will be taken seriously and makes it more likely they'll respond.

You can use this note to explain the purpose of the survey. For example, you might explain that the survey is part of a routine data collection process or that you're trying to analyze a specific problem.

You should also make it clear who will access or use the data. Explain how the process ensures confidentiality and, for example, that employees' immediate supervisors won't know who filled in the questionnaires.

3. Interviews

Whatever steps you take to ensure candid survey responses, some employees might still be uncomfortable about putting negative responses in writing. Face-to-face interviews are more likely to uncover employees' true opinions, if a skilled and neutral third party conducts them. Employees will be more open and interviewers will be able to probe employees' responses in more depth.

**Disadvantages of face-to-face interviews**

Because each employee has to be interviewed individually, conducting interviews is much more time consuming than using surveys. Interviewers have to be appropriately trained and spend a lot of time with each employee. Also, interviews don't enable employees to respond anonymously.

Disadvantages of using interviews are that they're more time consuming than surveys, interviewers must be appropriately trained, and some employees might not respond openly because there's no anonymity.

To avoid these pitfalls, you should plan the interview process carefully. As with surveys, you need to begin by determining exactly what information you want and then develop focused questions that are clear, precise, and easy to answer.

During interviews, you should give clear instructions to employees so that they know exactly what's expected of them.

Also explain who will use the information they provide and that anything they say will be kept confidential.

And it's important that interviewers have appropriate training. They should be skilled at putting nervous employees at ease, listening actively, asking probing questions, and summarizing information.

It's also a good idea to test the interview questions you design on a small number of employees first. You can then revise the questions if necessary – for example if some employees found them unclear – before conducting interviews on a company-wide scale.

Question

Match each scenario to the most appropriate method for gathering information from employees. More than one scenario may match to each method.

**Options:**

A.      You need to gather information about employees' opinions quickly so you can address high turnover across a department

B.      It's important to let employees comment anonymously on what they dislike about their departments and jobs

C.      You want to be able to probe employees' initial responses to ensure you understand the causes of any dissatisfaction

**Targets:**

1. Survey
2. Interview

Answer

*Surveys are a faster method of data collection than interviews and they enable employees to remain anonymous.*

*In face-to-face interviews, the interviewer can probe for more in-depth information, based on employees' initial responses. However, interviews are time consuming and don't enable employees to remain anonymous.*

4. Focus groups

Focus groups are discussion groups in which the members brainstorm to gather more in-depth information. They're useful when the reasons for talent departure aren't obvious from surveys or interviews – perhaps because the causes are too complex. You can also use them in conjunction with surveys and interviews to find solutions to the causes you identified. Typically, you involve a focus group in a series of discussions to obtain perceptions on a particular area of interest in a permissive, non-threatening environment.

Using focus groups has several advantages:

- subjective opinions – including conflicting ones – can be compared and debated until a group can reach a consensus
- through discussion, participants motivate each other

to come up with solutions
- group discussions yield more diverse and creative ideas
- they're inexpensive and don't take long to organize or conduct, and
- they can be used to explore a variety of issues

To get the most out of a focus group, you should get support from management, keep the focus group small, ensure the sample group is representative of the target group you're analyzing, and use facilitators to guide the discussion.

**Get support**

You should get support from management for focus groups so participants feel they're part of a legitimate, sanctioned process. If managers understand the advantages of these discussions, they'll have more confidence in the results.

**Keep group small**

A focus group will be most productive if you keep it small – about ten people. It needs to be small enough to manage properly so everyone gets a chance to contribute, but large enough that the ideas or opinions aired are diverse and informative.

**Ensure group is representative**

Participants in a focus group should represent the target population. Typically, a focus group is composed of individuals who are similar to each other in a way that's important to the person who sets up the group. For example, when using a focus group for turnover issues, the group may be homogenous in level of experience, rank, and influence in the organization. The question is, who can give you the type of information you need?

**Use facilitators**

You should use a facilitator to guide a focus group's discussion and keep the atmosphere relaxed and open. A facilitator helps keep the discussion focused on the problem, control overly aggressive participants, and encourage less outgoing people to contribute.

5. Nominal group technique

The nominal group technique is similar to the focus group method. You ask employees to discuss why others might be tempted to leave the organization, rather than why they themselves would leave. This shifts the employees' focus so the discussion no longer seems threatening. Employees are more likely to open up and disclose the real, underlying causes of talent departure if they're speaking about someone else.

As with the focus group method, this technique works best when you use neutral, third-party facilitators so employees know their input will be confidential and feel comfortable about speaking openly.

A representative sample of the target groups experiencing the highest turnover is selected to participate.

The group size is typically around 8 to 12. A small number of such groups may be used for large target groups.

So when using the nominal technique to find out about turnover, the facilitator would ask employees to list reasons why their colleagues have left or may leave. These lists are then revealed one by one and recorded. Similar list items are merged as appropriate.

Then employees prioritize the reasons and rate them by assigning points to each. The facilitator should emphasize that when assigning the rating, employees need to consider the issue that is causing the most turnover, rather than the one that may be most important to the employee.

After this, the top reasons are posted.

The nominal group technique is very efficient. You may be able to complete it in a one- to two-hour time frame, depending on the size of the group and the number of reasons given.

Trust is an important part of the process. This is established when employees realize their names will not be attached to any of the information or to the process itself.

## 6. Exit interviews

Exit interviews are perhaps the most common way for organizations to uncover the causes of turnover. These are done just before or after employees leave the organization. Exit interviews can take the form of face-to-face interviews, surveys, questionnaires, or even focus groups. An anonymous questionnaire is usually the most appropriate.

Question

Discovering the causes of resignations provides organizations with information they can use to improve staff retention.

What, do you think, is a disadvantage of the exit interview?

**Options:**

1. Respondents don't perceive the exit interview to have any benefits for them
2. The effort it takes to administer the exit interviews outweighs its benefits
3. Respondents who complete the exit interview may not raise personal issues that might have contributed to their departure
4. Answers to questions about what respondents think of the organization need to be evaluated in terms of personal bias

Answer

Because respondents don't feel there is any benefit for them to answering the questions of an exit interview, they may not return them, provide incomplete answers, or simply not answer truthfully.

But exit interviews are often unreliable. Questionnaires have a low return rate because people don't feel obligated to send their responses back to you. They've already moved on from the organization.

Respondents don't want to devote too much time and effort to a company they're not part of anymore. So those you do get back are often rushed or incomplete, which makes the data unreliable.

Some people aren't completely honest because they're worried what people will think of them. For example, someone might leave because of an unreasonable manager, but wouldn't say so for fear of getting a bad reference from the manager in future.

To make sure your exit interviews are successful, you need to establish trust and ensure employee confidentiality. It can also help to get departing employees to respond if you offer incentives and stress concern about colleagues.

**Establish trust**

You need to convince departing employees that you can be trusted to be discrete and to use the data you collect from them appropriately. If someone knows that former employees received bad references after being candid in their exit interviews, that person won't be completely honest.

**Ensure confidentiality**

Part of being trustworthy is keeping your promise that any information will be kept strictly confidential and anonymous. You should explain who will have access to the data. And using a third-party data collection source can help ensure anonymous input and show how the data is dealt with confidentially in reporting, use, and discussions.

**Offer incentives**

When employees leave, it can help to express your regret at their departure and to ask them to stay in touch. An open-door policy – where you let employees know that they're always welcome back – might encourage departing employees to offer constructive criticism.

You might even offer a small gift as an incentive for completing the questionnaire. Most people would feel guilty simply keeping the gift without returning the questionnaire.

### Stress concern about colleagues

It can sometimes be effective to appeal to departing employees' sense of responsibility for the colleagues they are leaving. You might ask a question like "How can we improve working conditions for those you're leaving behind?" This gives them an opportunity to influence conditions for friends who are staying.

All of these methods can be used to explore the causes of talent departure. If used well – even in conjunction where possible – you'll end up with a comprehensive list of specific reasons why employees leave your organization.

### Job Aid

Discovering Causes

**Purpose:** *Use this job aid to remind yourself of the different methods you can use to determine the causes of talent departure at your organization.*

There are five main ways you can gather information from employees to help determine the causes of talent departure.

### Surveys

You use surveys to test the prevailing attitudes or opinions of employees.

They should be

- simple and clear
- focused on specific issues
- submitted anonymously
- designed to allow comparison

### Interviews

You use interviews to get more in-depth information than surveys can provide.

To ensure a successful interview, you should

- ensure interviewers have appropriate training
- plan topics, questions, and the interview strategy carefully

- ensure employees know what to expect and that interview questions are clear
- test the interview design on a sample group before interviewing all relevant employees

**Focus groups**

You use focus groups to brainstorm ideas.

To be effective, a focus group should

- have the support of management
- consist of a small, manageable number of participants that accurately represent the target group of employees
- be guided by a trained facilitator

**The nominal group technique**

The nominal group technique is a structured group process that takes everyone's opinions into account. The benefit of the technique is that the group shares and discusses all issues before evaluation. When evaluation occurs, each participant "nominates" his or her priority issues, and then ranks these using an agreed-upon scale.

This technique works best when you

- use neutral, third-party facilitators
- keep information confidential and anonymous
- keep group size relatively small – 8 to 12 people

**Exit interviews**

You use exit interviews to collect data from employees who are leaving an organization, to determine their reasons for leaving.

You'll get more input from departing employees if you

- convince employees that you can be trusted to keep whatever information they provide confidential
- use incentives to raise the response rate when questionnaires are used

- stress your concern for the colleagues they are leaving behind

Question

Match each scenario to the most appropriate method for gathering information about the possible causes of talent departures.

**Options:**

A. You meet with employees one at a time to get their opinions about the possible causes of talent departures

B. You collect data from many employees in a short time

C. You get representatives from departments to discuss creative solutions for talent departures

D. You ask a group of employees to list reasons why people leave the organization

E. You talk to a person who's resigned to find out why he decided to go

**Targets:**

1. Interview
2. Survey
3. Focus group
4. Nominal group technique
5. Exit interview

Answer

*In face-to-face interviews, a skilled interviewer can probe employees' initial responses to uncover more detailed and candid information about possible reasons for talent departures.*

*Surveys are faster and cheaper than other methods, so they're best for collecting large amounts of data.*

*You can use a focus group to involve representative employees in discussing a complex problem that's resulting in talent departures and in finding creative solutions to it.*

*Using the nominal group technique, you ask employees to list reasons their colleagues might leave. This makes the technique less threatening than other methods, so employees are more likely to discuss their opinions openly.*

*Through an exit interview, you capture a specific employee's stated reasons for leaving the organization.*

7. Summary

Determining the causes of talent departure in a specific organization involves gathering information from employees. To do this, you can use anonymous surveys, face-to-face interviews, focus groups, the nominal group technique, and exit interviews. Once you've identified causes, you can take steps to address them.

**Follow-on Activity**

Creating a Retention Survey

**Purpose:** *Use this follow-on activity to create a survey for determining the causes of talent departures in your organization.*

**Instructions for use:** To use this tool, decide what questions you need to ask employees to elicit specific information about why they would consider leaving your organization.

For example, you might want to know how employees feel about

- their job security
- your organization's leadership style
- work schedule flexibility
- opportunities to succeed at work
- opportunities to acquire new skills
- whether there are adequate resources to complete their tasks efficiently and well
- stress levels in the workplace
- satisfaction with salary
- relationships with coworkers
- relationships with managers

- perceptions of the work
- individual recognition

# STRATEGIES FOR TALENT RETENTION

1. Retention through job satisfaction

As a manager or supervisor, your relationship with employees is a key factor in whether your organization retains talent. Put simply, people leave managers and supervisors more often than they leave companies or jobs. And anything you do that makes employees feel undervalued is likely to contribute to higher turnover.

So it's important to be a considerate manager. You need to be interested in and respectful toward your employees, and know how to supervise without micromanaging them.

To keep talent, you also need to know and be supportive of employees' own priorities and career aspirations.

Above all, you can help prevent talented employees from leaving when you ensure their jobs are satisfying.

As a manager, you can improve employees' job satisfaction – and so retain talented employees – by using four main strategies:

- communicate the link between employees' work and your organization's success
- provide employees with constructive feedback
- be willing to give talented employees sufficient autonomy, and
- provide employees with growth and development opportunities

2. Communicate the link

For employees to be satisfied in their jobs and happy to stay with an organization, they need to know what role they play in its success. As a manager, you need to communicate this to them. You should ensure they know what the organization's mission and key objectives are – and understand that it's these that their work supports.

**When to communicate objectives**

It's important to explain what your organization's mission and objectives are to new employees when they begin their employment. In addition, though, you should communicate any changes in the organization's mission or objectives to all employees when they occur, and ensure that employees are constantly aware of their roles in attaining organizational objectives.

For instance, a key strategic objective of a car manufacturer is to develop more environmentally friendly cars and processes.

Managers in various departments, including Design and Production, explain how employees contribute to this objective.

Their conversations include how using recycled materials in car designs, as well as how recycling materials during production, contributes to the objective. They also discuss the importance of coming up with innovative green designs and processes, and how seemingly unrelated, small tasks contribute to the company's success in meeting this objective.

You can inspire and motivate employees by connecting the organization's mission and objectives to their jobs. And when you're able to communicate an exciting description of the organization's future, you encourage employees to make it happen. It's also important for you to model the commitment and the level of engagement you want employees to mirror. Remember, it's your role as manager to give them a good reason to be dedicated to your organization.

Part of communicating how employees' work is linked to organizational success is developing meaningful goals for them – ones that clearly advance organizational strategy. Then you can tie appropriate measurement and reward systems to those goals.

To clearly communicate what's expected of each of your employees, it helps to create performance agreements in which you specify expectations and methods of measuring performance.

A key part of creating a performance agreement is to ask employees for their input. That's because if they're involved in developing the terms of these agreements, they're far more likely to accept them.

You may set performance expectations in relation to several factors:

- the quantity of work produced by an employee
- the quality of the employee's work
- the time it takes to complete work, and
- the costs associated with the employee's work

## Quantity

Quantity expectations may, for example, be measured in terms of number of customer problems resolved per month, number of outbound sales calls made per day, or number of hours lost as a result of absenteeism over a certain period of time.

## Quality

Quality expectations could be measured in terms of number of client complaints received per month, percentage of voluntary staff resignations, or percentage of work returned for correction of errors.

## Time

Time expectations could be measured using number of customer calls missed per shift, number of client deadlines not met, or percentage of complaints resolved successfully in a certain time period.

## Cost

Cost expectations might be measured in terms of money saved

over a previous period, or number of hours to finish a task each time.

Job satisfaction is partly related to how clearly you know what's expected of you.

Unclear or continuously changing expectations may keep people on edge and create unhealthy stress.

So to retain top talent, you need to set clear expectations and link these to organizational success. This gives employees a sense of purpose.

Question

Which are effective ways to communicate the link employees have to an organization?

**Options:**

1. Relay your organization's mission and primary goals to all staff
2. Communicate changes in company objectives to staff on a quarterly basis
3. Set meaningful and specific objectives for all staff members
4. Encourage staff to accept performance agreements that you've drawn up for them independently

Answer

**Option 1:** *This is a correct option. To foster job satisfaction, it's essential that employees are aware of your organization's mission and key objectives, and how their work supports these.*

**Option 2:** *This option is incorrect. To retain talent, managers should always communicate changes in an organization's mission or objectives. These changes affect employees' roles in attaining organizational objectives.*

**Option 3:** *This option is correct. If employees have meaningful goals and these are tied to appropriate measurement and reward systems, they're likely to have better job satisfaction.*

**Option 4:** *This is an incorrect option. Part of retaining talent and creating job satisfaction is creating performance agreements. Employees should participate in this process to ensure they'll accept the agreements.*

3. Provide constructive feedback

It's important to build and nurture good relationships with your employees.

This helps improve employee job satisfaction and is key in retaining employees.

One of the ways that you can help establish and maintain positive relationships with employees is by providing regular, constructive feedback.

Feedback is important for employees because it helps them answer four basic questions: "Where is the organization heading?" "How will we get there?" "How do you expect me to contribute?", and "How am I doing?"

The answers to these questions help provide much of what gives meaning to an employee's efforts and engagement.

You need to give feedback to make sure employees' efforts stay aligned with organizational goals and your expectations.

To provide feedback that's constructive and that improves talented employees' job satisfaction, you should follow certain guidelines:

- deliver the feedback immediately – make sure it's not delayed or it will be less effective
- discuss specific negative and positive behavior or attitudes and back up what you say with facts
- be explicit about what actions the employee can take to improve and about expectations for this person's future performance, and
- reaffirm the importance of the employee's work to your team, department, and organization

Jessica is a manager working for an advertising and design company. She reviews a magazine advertisement that Megan produced for one of the company's biggest clients. Normally Megan produces work that's on time and of exceptionally good quality. However, this time she submits the advertisement three days after the final deadline and it doesn't meet the client's stipulated requirements.

Jessica's not too sure how she should approach Megan, so she gets someone else to fix the advertisement up while she thinks about what she should say to her.

Two weeks later, after the client approves the revised advertisement, Jessica sets up a meeting with Megan to discuss the project.

Follow along as Jessica gives feedback to Megan.

> Jessica: Thanks for meeting with me Megan. I'd like to discuss the advertisement you produced about two weeks ago.
>
> Megan: Two weeks ago? Oh yes, I remember that. It was a magazine advertisement, right?
>
> Jessica: Yes, that's the one I'm referring to. Besides submitting it three days after the deadline, the work was really shoddy.
>
> Megan: It was? I didn't realize that. Nobody said anything until now.
>
> Jessica: I'm used to you producing work of better quality. The advertisement just didn't meet the client's requirements and I'm disappointed.
>
> Megan: I know it was late but that's because there was a problem with the printers. But what specifically was wrong with the advertisement? I read through the client's brief and worked according to the requirements.
>
> Jessica: I don't really have time to go through the specifics with you and I shouldn't really have to. I just need you to understand that what you produced wasn't acceptable.

Question

What do you think of the feedback Jessica gives to Megan?

**Options:**

1. Jessica gives Megan good, constructive feedback that's to the point
2. Jessica's feedback isn't constructive and doesn't help to build a positive relationship with Megan
3. Jessica's feedback isn't constructive, but in this case, it's more important for Jessica to demonstrate her authority effectively

Answer

Jessica's feedback isn't constructive. She doesn't give Megan specific details about what she did wrong, doesn't reaffirm her value to the team, and doesn't tell Megan how she can improve. Moreover, she waited too long to give Megan the feedback.

Because Jessica's feedback is more negative than constructive, it may actually harm her relationship with Megan. It's also likely to decrease Megan's job satisfaction – and if it continues, it could lead to Megan leaving the company.

Employees' job satisfaction – and the likelihood they'll stay with an organization – is also affected by how well managers recognize, acknowledge, and praise employees' efforts.

Recognition, acknowledgement, and praise are important tools for retention, and can often be more significant than monetary rewards.

They boost morale and increase job satisfaction. Through them, employees learn how managers feel about their performance.

But many managers give praise and recognition to employees only for work they consider to be excellent or outstanding.

This type of praise is important, but more consistent expression of appreciation goes a long way toward contributing to high performance and talent retention.

It can enhance employees' sense of satisfaction with work, supervisors, colleagues, and their place of employment.

Like other types of feedback, praise should be specific, offered immediately after the exceptional action, and given in person.

Question

Which are effective ways to provide feedback in a way that fosters job satisfaction and ultimately helps retain talented employees?

**Options:**

1. Deliver praise only after an employee has done outstanding work
2. Give feedback right after a situation occurs and be specific and factual about the relevant behavior or attitude
3. Describe clearly the actions the employee can take to improve and the expectations for this person's future performance
4. Tell employees that if they don't hear from you, it means they're doing alright
5. Show employees you appreciate their hard work by acknowledging and recognizing it through praise

Answer

*Option 1:* This is an incorrect option. The consistent expression of appreciation goes a long way toward contributing to high performance and talent retention.

*Option 2:* This option is correct. For feedback to be effective, it needs to be given right away. It should also be specific and factual about the relevant behavior or attitude, so the employee knows what to avoid in future.

*Option 3:* This option is correct. Constructive feedback provides explicit information about what actions the employee needs to take to improve and about expectations for future performance. This helps keep employee objectives aligned with those of the organization and encourages the employee to perform better.

*Option 4:* This option is incorrect. It's important to acknowledge and *praise employees' efforts regularly, as well as to provide constructive criticism if problems arise.*

**Option 5**: *This option is correct. Praise, acknowledgement, and recognition are important tools for retention and can often be more significant than monetary rewards.*

4. Give autonomy

Giving talented employees autonomy involves trusting them to work independently and to use their own judgment about how to complete required work. It also involves letting them know they have management's support for decisions they make. This empowers employees, adding to their job satisfaction and thereby helping you to retain them.

Giving talented employees more control over how they do their work often results in their taking more responsibility for the quality of the work they produce. For an organization, this can mean that better products or services are produced.

Allowing employees independence can also improve their decision-making and problem-solving skills.

So giving talented employees autonomy can have several benefits for an organization, in addition to making it more likely that their talent will be retained.

Some managers struggle to give their employees enough autonomy.

This may be because they feel the need to stay in control of employees' work.

In other instances, it's simply a case of a manager thinking that by doing employees' work for them, they're helping out. But this can offend employees and make them feel less valued.

Managers may also be reluctant to give autonomy to employees for other reasons:

- they enjoy particular work themselves, and don't want to give it to others to do
- they're under the impression that employees don't

- want more responsibility or independence
- they fear employees are more competent and may perform better than them, or
- they may think the idea of empowerment being beneficial is just a passing phase

Delia, a magazine editor, tells her team of writers they can approach their writing assignments from any angle and can use any style of writing that's appropriate.

The only conditions are that they write about the topics they're assigned and meet their deadlines.

By giving her writers the flexibility to use their creativity while still setting certain boundaries, Delia ensures the writers feel trusted, in control of their work, and eager to produce work of high quality.

Question

Which are appropriate ways to give talented employees more autonomy?

**Options:**

1. Allow some autonomy, but stay in control behind the scenes and help out when you think an employee is in trouble
2. Give employees permission to implement their own decisions after checking them with you
3. Provide employees with opportunities to use their own judgment
4. Let the employees know that management supports their independent decisions

Answer

**Option 1:** *This option is incorrect. Allowing autonomy means giving your employees control. If you're staying in control behind the scenes, you haven't let go and your employees will recognize your efforts as superficial. This won't help build trust with employees.*

***Option 2:*** *This is an incorrect option. Giving autonomy means giving employees the independence to make decisions about the way they do their work – rather than checking their decisions.*

***Option 3:*** *This is a correct option. Giving autonomy to employees means giving them the independence to use their own judgment about how they do their jobs.*

***Option 4:*** *This option is correct. If employees know they have the trust and support of management, they're likely to be more confident and satisfied in their jobs.*

5. Provide development opportunities

Another strategy for ensuring job satisfaction – and ultimately talent retention – is helping talented employees develop their skills and careers.

As a manager, doing this demonstrates that you have a sincere interest in your employees' welfare, so it helps in building a solid relationship of trust between you and your employees.

Highly motivated and talented employees are likely to become bored if they're not given opportunities to develop.

As well as helping them achieve their career goals, you need to ensure they feel challenged within your organization.

To help talented employees develop their careers, you should assess and remain aware of their development needs, create individual development plans, offer coaching and mentoring, give stretch assignments, and provide structured training and development options.

**Assess needs**

It's natural for talented employees to outgrow their positions and to want new challenges and opportunities to develop their skills.

A good manager is aware of this and should respond appropriately by helping employees determine what needs to be done for them to achieve their career goals. This prevents talented employees from getting bored and ensures they remain satisfied in their jobs.

## Create development plans

As a manager, it's vital to develop individual development plans with talented employees. A development plan identifies an employee's career goals and the steps that should be taken to achieve those goals.

If talented employees feel that by working for your organization, they're moving closer to achieving their goals, they're far more likely to stay with the organization.

## Offer coaching and mentoring

Coaching talented employees can help them develop and advance in their careers. This involves providing constant feedback, communicating with individuals and the team about problems, and recommending ways to improve and advance.

Mentoring goes hand-in-hand with coaching. While coaching focuses on learning and development, mentoring focuses on guiding and nurturing individual employees.

## Give stretch assignments

To help talented employees expand their existing skills or learn new skills, you should provide them with assignments that challenge them. These are referred to as stretch assignments. They should be suited to employees' abilities, but also challenge them in areas that may be new to them.

## Provide training and development options

Providing talented employees with structured training and development can motivate them to stay with your organization.

For instance, you might send talented employees on learning courses outside the organization or set up internal training courses. The key is to provide employees with various training and development options.

Making sure that talented employees have access to the tools for developing their careers is important because it encourages

TALENT MANAGEMENT

them to take charge of their own progress.

One way of doing this is to create a career center. This is either a physical or online center that provides resources and assists people in assessing and planning their careers.

Career centers may offer counseling to employees, information regarding the availability of jobs within and outside your organization, and tests for assessing skills, talents, interests, and motivation. Talented employees may use these resources to evaluate their career decisions.

Question

In which ways can a manager provide growth and development opportunities that encourage talented employees to stay with an organization?

**Options:**

1. Whenever possible, ensure employees work on their own
2. Provide the employees with in-house training
3. Work with the employees to identify their career goals and steps for achieving them
4. Assign more senior employees to provide ongoing teaching, guidance, and support
5. Assign the employees more work than usual so they feel challenged
6. Give the employees work that challenges them
7. Continuously assess the employees' development needs

Answer

**Option 1:** *This is an incorrect option. It's important to give talented employees sufficient autonomy, but this doesn't mean they can't work on teams. Also, this doesn't necessarily involve giving them opportunities to develop.*

**Option 2:** *This option is correct. To help talented employees develop* their careers with your organization, you should make training and development opportunities available to them.

**Option 3:** *This is a correct option. Creating individual development plans for talented employees is one way to demonstrate that they can develop their careers at your organization.*

**Option 4:** *This option is correct. Coaching and mentoring are effective ways to give talented employees the opportunity to develop at your organization.*

**Option 5:** *This option is incorrect. It's important to challenge talented employees, but putting undue pressure on them isn't a way to encourage them to stay with your organization.*

**Option 6:** *This is a correct option. Stretch assignments – or assignments that challenge talented employees – can help them develop their skills and prevent them from becoming bored.*

**Option 7:** *This option is correct. A manager should monitor talented employees to determine when they're outgrowing their current positions and need opportunities to*

6. Summary

To retain talented employees, it's vital that managers have good relationships with them. Managers can also take several steps to improve the job satisfaction of these employees, making it less likely they'll leave an organization.

These steps include communicating the link between these employees' work and the organization's success; providing ongoing, constructive feedback; giving the employees sufficient autonomy; and providing them with opportunities for growth and development.

**Job Aid**

Retaining Talent

**Purpose:** *Use this job aid to review the strategies managers should use to retain talent.*

There are four strategies managers can use to retain talent.

**Communicate the link**

Managers should ensure that talented employees know how their work contributes to an organization's success, and what the organization's vision and objectives are.

They should also ensure that employees know and agree about what's expected of them. It can be helpful for this reason to involve employees in drawing up clear performance agreements, which outline performance expectations and how they can be measured.

**Provide constructive feedback**

Managers can build trust with talented employees and contribute to their job satisfaction by providing ongoing, constructive feedback.

For feedback to be effective

- it should be delivered as soon as possible after the relevant behavior
- it should be used to address specific positive and negative aspects of employees' work and behavior, drawing on facts
- when negative performance is addressed, it should include specific actions employees can take to improve and a clear indication of what will be expected in future
- it should end by affirming the employee's importance to the team, department, and organization

**Give autonomy**

Giving talented employees autonomy involves empowering them to make their own decisions about how to complete required work, and supporting these decisions. This adds to the employees' sense of responsibility, and can improve their levels of satisfaction with their jobs.

**Provide development opportunities**

Providing talented employees with challenges and opportunities to develop their skills is an effective way of improving their job satisfaction and encouraging them to stay with your organization.

To help talented employees develop, you should

- continually assess and remain aware of their development needs, and provide opportunities for development when it's clear they're outgrowing their current positions and need new challenges
- create a career development plan with each employee, outlining the employee's career goals and steps for achieving them
- offer coaching and mentoring to assist employees in acquiring new skills
- provide stretch assignments that challenge employees
- provide a variety of structured training and development options

www.ingramcontent.com/pod-product-compliance
Lightning Source LLC
Chambersburg PA
CBHW071453220526
45472CB00003B/779